Bella Mangiare

"Beautiful Eating"

Italian Cooking Fresh & Easy

Bella Mangiare

"Beautiful Eating"

Rosalie Schwamb

ReadersMagnet, LLC

Published in the United States of America
ISBN Paperback: 978-1-949981-00-1
ISBN eBook: 978-1-949981-01-8

ReadersMagnet, LLC
10620 Treena Street, Suite 230 | San Diego, California, 92131 USA
1.619.354.2643 | www.readersmagnet.com

Book design copyright © 2018 by ReadersMagnet, LLC. All rights reserved.
Cover design by Ericka Walker
Interior design by Shemaryl Evans
Photo by Rick Schwamb & Andy Match

$\mathcal{A}$cknowledgements

I owe my deepest gratitude to my mother Josephine (the Mediterranean) for believing in me.

I want to thank my wonderful husband Mark and children Mark II and
Rosalia for their patients and faithful support in writing this book.

My Nanu Jerome and Nana Rosalie LaVora for the teaching to my soul.

My Pena Joanna LaVora Lemke, My Zia MaryAnn LaVora Sentell, My Zia Jalina
Woelky for sticking by my side and picking me up when I was down.

My American Family Insurance Company, family.

My friend Shelly Hart Grimme, for all her great advice and style.

All my Familia for rooting me every step of the way.

Rick Schwamb (Photographer) Front page.

Jan Kaster (Angell Park Senior Apartments)

Contents

$\mathcal{T}$ips to my readers

Proper way to prepare a recipe:

Read the entire recipe—this is very important.
Gather ingredients and make sure you have them all.
Gather all supplies needed.
Take butter and eggs out of refridgerator so the butter can soften and eggs can
     warm up to room temp.
Preheat your oven, if baking, just before mixing.
Prepare ingredients, cut, chop or sauté.

Lists:

Before food shopping I make a list and number 1 2 3 4
1 = When you first walk in, fruits, vegetables, and breads.
2 = In the back of the store, meats and lunch meats.
3 = Middle of the store canned goods and pasta
4 = Left of the store eggs, milk and frozen foods.
Food shopping will go faster and you will be more organized and buy just what you
     came for in most cases, unless you are with someone like my husband.

Decreasing your fat intake

You can lower you cholesterol level and decrease risk of heart disease by cutting your fat consumption.
· When called in the recipe to fry, you can bake or even broil.
· Choose lean meats, making sure to cut off the fat before cooking.
· Try not to eat luncheon meats and eat sausage and bacon sparingly.
· Remove the skin from poultry, if possible.
· Use olive oil and a tab of butter instead of heavy oils.
· Season with herbs.
· Use low-fat milk products such as buttermilk, fat free milk or skim milk.

Conversions & Equivalencies

1 pinch = less than ⅛ teaspoon (dry)
1 dash = 3 drops to ¼ teaspoon (liquid)
3 teaspoons = 1 tablespoon = ½ ounce (liquid and dry)
2 tablespoons = 1 ounce (liquid and dry)
4 tablespoons = 2 ounces (liquid and dry) = ¼ cup
5 ⅓ tablespoons = ⅓ cup
16 tablespoons = 8 ounces = 1 cup = ½ pound
16 tablespoons = 48 teaspoons
32 tablespoons = 16 ounces = 2 cups = 1 pound
64 tablespoons = 32 ounces = 1 quart = 2 pounds
1 cup = 8 ounces (liquid) = ½ pint
2 cups = 16 ounces (liquid) = 1 pint
4 cups = 32 ounces (liquid) = 2 pints = 1 quart
16 cups = 128 ounces (liquid) = 4 quarts = 1 gallon
1 quart = 2 pints (dry)
8 quarts = 1 peck (dry)
4 pecks = 1 bushel (dry)

Quantities to serve 100 people

Coffee: 3 pounds
Cream: 3 quarts
Milk: 6 gallons
Soup: 5 gallons
Ham: 40 pounds
Beef: 40 pounds
Roast and Pork: 40 pounds
Chicken: 40 pounds
Potatoes: 35 pounds
Vegetables: 10 cans
Baked beans: 5 gallons
Bread: 10 loafs

Rolls: 200
Butter: 3 pounds
Potatoes salad: 12 quarts
Fruit salad: 20 quarts
Vegetable salad: 20 quarts
Lettuce: 20 heads
Dressings: 3 quarts
Pies: 18
Cakes: 8
Ice cream: 4 gallons
Cheese: 3 pounds
Olives: 1 ¾ pounds

$\mathcal{H}$erbs

Salt and Pepper used throughout the book means: 3 shakes of salt/3 shakes of pepper or to your liking. When I state Italian herbs throughout the book in the recipes, my mix is below.

Just use what the recipe calls for and store the remaining in tight sealed plastic bag.
1 tbsp dried oregano
1 tbsp dried basil
1 tbsp dried rosemary
1 tbsp dried thyme
1 tbsp dried sage
1 tbsp dried marjoram

Basil—Has a sweet flavor it is used in sauces, pizzas, salads and pasta dishes. It is also the main ingredient used in pesto. Great as a garnish on any pasta dishes. I use throughout the book often and it is the staple of our family cooking.

Bay Leaf—Has a pungent flavor, add a bay leaf or two to marinades, stocks, stews, good in soups and meat dishes for slow cooking remove before serving.

Cilantro—Used in soups, stews, chicken and rice, salads, tomato based sauces and as a garnish. Use sparingly this gives everything a kick and fresh flavor to salads.

Fennel—Has a sweet and hot flavor used in sauces, meats and sausage also great used in marinades.

Oregano or Marjoram—Has a strong aromatic odor well with vegetables, roast beef, lamb, chicken and pork

Parsley—Used in soups, pasta and vegetable dishes as well as sauces. Goes well with fish, poultry, veal and pork. Use fresh leaves as garnish. This is another herb I used daily in almost everything.

Rosemary—Blend well with garlic and thyme to season lamb roasts, meat stews, fish and poultry dishes, tomato sauces, and vegetables.

Sage—Used in stuffing, pork, lamb, meats, and sausages. Chopped leaves flavor salads, also rubbed sparingly on chicken with paprika.

Thyme—It is often used in soups and sauces, with meat, poultry or fish. Fresh thyme has the most flavor used whole, with the stem.

My Nanu Jerome, my heart my heart, and Nana Rosalie, a true lady,
in there garden where they loved to spend time together.

Appetizers

Mediterranean Wraps

1 cup sweet Italian sausages, chopped and cooked

½ cup black beans

¼ cup red onions, chopped small

2 tablespoons basil, chopped fine

1 teaspoon salt

¼ cup green peppers, chopped fine

1 clove garlic, minced

22 wonton wrappers

Marinara sauce (any kind)

Mix all the ingredients. Lightly brush water over all four edges of the wonton wrapper.

Spread 1 tbsp of filling along one edge of the wrapper, roll up tightly and repeat with remaining wrappers.

Place on baking sheet coated with cooking spray. Lightly spray wrappers.

Bake at 375 for 15 minutes until goldenbrown, serve warm with marinara sauce.

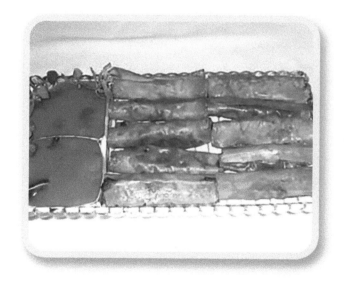

Food for Thought:
We wanted to make it with less fat so we baked them.

My mom and I enjoyed coming up with this recipe.

Family Favorite

Serve Mangiare

ROSALIE SCHWAMB

Cheese Olive Snacks

2 cups cheese, any kind, shredded (preferred mozzarella)

½ cup olives any kind

½ cup mayonnaise

⅓ cup green onions chopped

Cracker, any kind

In bowl, combine all ingredients.

Place a teaspoon of mixture on cracker and place on ungreased baking sheet.

Bake at 375 for 7 minutes, serve hot.

This is an easy "make ahead" mixture and before guests even sit down place on crackers and in the oven for 7 minutes and done.

Serve Mangiare

$\mathcal{M}$ a Schwamb's Onion Dip

2 packages cream cheese, softened
4 tablespoons milk

1 small onion, chopped

Mix all the ingredients.
Serve with potato chips
Add more milk if it's not loose enough.

Fond Memories
*My daughter Rosalia's favorite, when she would go
visit grandma.
They would put in the movie Beauty
and the Beast and have chip dip.*

*Serve
Mangiare*

ROSALIE SCHWAMB

*B*eef Pockets

8 oz sweet Italian sausage, cooked

1 cup pepperoni, chopped

¾ cup onions, chopped

¾ cup green peppers, chopped

¾ cup mushrooms, any kind, chopped (optional)

4 ounces cream cheese

2 packages 13.oz pizza dough (also can make your own)

1 egg

Parmesan cheese, shredded

2 cups pizza sauce

In skillets, cook sausage, onion and green pepper.

Take off heat and add the pepperoni, cream cheese and some parmesan cheese.

Grease 2 large baking sheets, roll out dough on floured surface, cut 3 by 3 inch squares.

Place 1 tbsp of mixture and close like a pocket, seal with fork. When all are pocketed, brush with egg.

Bake at 425 for about 12 minutes.

Home Run with my Kids!

SERVE WITH:
Pizza or Marinara Sauce

Serve Mangiare

Garlic Dip

1 small red onions, chopped

1 teaspoon garlic, minced

1 teaspoon oregano

¼ teaspoon salt

1 cup mayonnaise

1 cup sour cream

1 lb sourdough bread, round, unsliced (or any kind of round bread)

Mix all ingredients, put in fridge.

Cut off top of round bread and hollow out bottom, leaving shell.

Place cubed bread around the shell of the bread and put filling in the shell.

Serve.

Passed down from my Aunt Mary-Ann's Kitchen

This can also be used as a dip with chips garlic salt instead of minced and omit the oregano.

Courtney and Jeromes Family Favorite

Serve Mangiare

ROSALIE SCHWAMB

Salsa

1 med white onion, chopped

1 med jalapeño pepper, chopped

4 med tomatoes, chopped

¼ cup cilantro, chopped

Salt and pepper

1 clove garlic, minced

¼ cup tomato sauce if you dont want too much heat

Chop all fresh vegetables fine, and then add salt and
pepper to your taste,
and then you can either add chopped
fresh garlic, or powder garlic.

If too hot, add about ¼ cup of the 6-oz can of tomato sauce.

Hint - you can add 1 cup
of mango and 1 cup of
strawberries to this recipe,
and serve with tortilla chips.
WOW, WHAT A
HOME RUN.

COUSIN RICK'S
FAMILY FAVORITE

*Serve
Mangiare*

*I*talian Stuffed Portabello

1 pound Italian Sausage chopped and browned

2 large cloves garlic, minced

2 teaspoons fresh basil, chopped

2 teaspoons fresh oregano, chopped

½ cup mascarpone cheese

½ cup Parmesan cheese or you can use gorgonzola

¾ cup bread crumbs

6 to 8 portabella mushrooms, steam and cleaned out well

¼ cup mozzarella cheese for the topping of the mushrooms

Place mushrooms on baking sheet or any shallow pan and brush with olive oil inside and out.

Mix all ingredients and fill mushrooms.

Top with mozzarella cheese.

Bake at 350 until cheese melts, about 10 to 15 min.

Great with:
Any main dish also with any pasta dish. Or by itself with a salad and some good wine.

Merlot

Serve Mangiare

Rosalie Schwamb

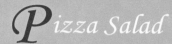 Pizza Salad

1 thin crusted Italian bread shell or pizza shell

8 oz of spinch dip

1 cup chopped broccoli

1 cup cubed cook turkey or chicken

½ cup red onion chopped

2 tomatoes cubed

Spread the spinach over the baked shell.

Top with all the rest of the ingredients and serve.

Great Easy Meal

This is a great dish to bring to parties.
It feeds alot and is great cold.
PARTY FAVORITE

Serve
Mangiare

Caponata (Caponadina) Eggplant Salad

10 eggplants, cut into 1 inch cubes

2 cups celery sliced very thinly

1 ½ cups of boiling water

1 ¾ cups of oil

4 onions, very thinly sliced

1 cup tomato paste

1 tablespoon of cocoa

1 cup Sicilian olives, chopped

¼ cup of capers

½ cup sugar

½ cup balsamic vinegar

¾ cup pine nuts

Salt and pepper

Place the eggplant and celery in a bowl of boiling water, shut off heat, add salt and let sit for about a ½ hour then drain. Rinse well.

In sauté pan, with half the oil, sauté eggplant, onions after lightly browned. Then place on paper towel.

In same sauté pan, put in the rest of the oil and, on low heat, put in the tomato paste, olives, capers, sugar, and vinegar. Sauté for about 5 minutes on simmer then add the cocoa, salt and pepper. Put in the eggplant mixture and let sit for about 1 hour then place into small jars.

Makes about 10 cups.

Store in fridge. Can be enjoyed right away or stored in fridge for 3 months.

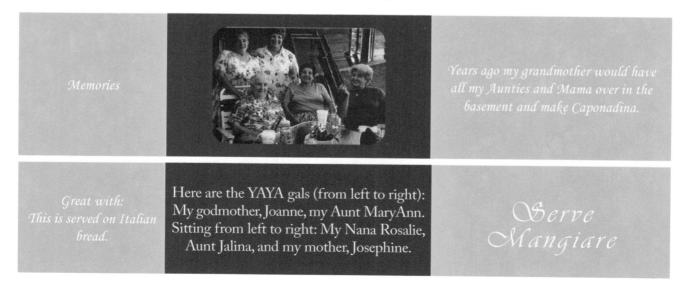

Memories

Years ago my grandmother would have all my Aunties and Mama over in the basement and make Caponadina.

Great with:
This is served on Italian bread.

Here are the YAYA gals (from left to right): My godmother, Joanne, my Aunt MaryAnn. Sitting from left to right: My Nana Rosalie, Aunt Jalina, and my mother, Josephine.

Serve Mangiare

Eggplant Parmesan

1 eggplant peeled, very large or 2 medium ones

1 tablespoon butter

½ cup olive oil pour in just half with butter at first then see if more is needed

2 teaspoons mixed Italian herbs

1 small onion chopped

1 tablespoon garlic chopped

¾ cup Parmesan cheese

1 cup bread crumbs

2 eggs

¾ cup mozzarella cheese

2 cups marinara sauce recipe found in the book

Slice the eggplant, dip in egg and then bread in Italian herbs, garlic, parmesan and bread crumbs. Saute in skillet for about 5 minutes with olive oil, butter, onion and garlic.

In 8 X 11 backing pan, place the eggplant and layer with parmesan cheese.

Then put the marinara sauce over the eggplant and the mozzarella cheese.

Bake 350 for 15 min or until the cheeses melt.

Great with:
Great served with a salad or meat dish.

Serve
Mangiare

My Olive Tapenade

20 pitted Kalamata olives, chopped

½ teaspoon of anchovy paste (optional)

1 tablespoon capers, chopped

1 tablespoon Italian parsley (optional)

Pepper

Combine all ingredients together, served over crusted crostini, Italian bread.

Cut the bread into 2x2 inch squares and place the mixture on top with some parmesan cheese.

Make ahead the mixture and store in fridge.
Tips

Cousin Marie's
FAMILY FAVORITE

Serve Mangiare

Rosalie Schwamb

Breads

Garlic Bread (Pane)

1 large Italian bread, sliced into
8 big slices

1 cup butter, softened

2 tablespoons garlic powder

½ cup Parmesan cheese

2 tablespoons parsley, finely chopped

2 large tomatoes, cut into 8 slices

Mix the butter, garlic and parmesan cheese.

Spread on the slices of bread. Add the parsley and slice of tomato.

Drizzle with olive oil. Broil until light brown.

Passed Down From:
My Godmother (Pena)
Joann's Kitchen

My Pena with my son Mark

The tomatoes and
parsley are optional

Serve
Mangiare

Pizza Dough My Way

1 cup warm water

1 package active dry yeast

½ teaspoon sugar

1 ½ tablespoon olive oil

2 ½ cups flour

½ cup cornmeal

2 teaspoon sea salt

In bowl, stir the water, yeast and sugar then let sit until foamy looking, about 10 min.

Stir 1 ½ tbsp olive oil, 2 ½ cups flour, ½ cup cornmeal, and the salt. Mix until forms a ball.

Then knead on floured surface, about 10 min.

Then lightly oil large bowl, put in the dough. Turn bowl to oil the dough, cover with plastic wrap. Spray the wrap before covering the dough. Put bowl in warm place for an hour.

Then gently knead the dough and divide into 2 pieces. Roll each piece on floured surface into rectangle and place on cookie sheet. Blind bake until lightly browned. Bake at 475.

Then pour sauce on crust then top with all your favorite ingredients, finish baking until done. Then add olive oil and salt.

My work family favorite
Thanks Hock, Jill and Shel for all your ra ra's.
Oh and Hock I know I have a standing invitation to show you how to make my pizza. Be right over!

BELLA MANGIARE - BEAUTIFUL EATING

27

Stuff Sicilian Bread

8 ounces sweet Italian sausages (Can subsitute for bacon)

1 cup potatoes peeled

2 cloves garlic chopped

½ package fresh spinach

1 cup cheddar cheese (Sub any cheese.)

1 medium onion chopped

1 package of bread dough

Saute sausage until brown, set aside. Pan fry potatoes, onions, garlic salt and pepper.

Roll out the bread with some flour, brush the rolled bread with some olive oil.

Place the spinach, sausage, potatoes mixture, and cheese in the rolled out bread dough.

Roll and press in sides, brush with egg.

Bake 350 degrees until med brown, about 30 minutes.

Uncle Cork, Uncle Tim, and Uncle Howard
FAMILY FAVORITE

Serves: 6-8

Serve Mangiare

Rosalie Schwamb

$\mathcal{A}$sparagus (di pane) Flat Bread

1 cup of onions, chopped

2 cloves garlic, minced

3 tablespoons butter

1 pound asparagus spears, fresh, cut into pieces

1 ½ cup green bell peppers, chopped

¼ teaspoon pepper

2 8-oz cans of crescent roll dough

1 cup mozzarella cheese, shredded

1 cup Swiss cheese, shredded

In saute pan, cook onion and garlic until tender with a tablespoon of butter and a little olive oil.

Add asparagus and peppers, saute until tender, then add pepper.

Press dough into ungreased baking pan, seal all seams.

Bake at 375 for 7 to 9 minutes or until lightly browned.

Top with asparagus and peppers, sprinkle the cheese all over.

Bake 7 to 8 minutes longer. Cut into squares.

| Serves: 6-8 | Classic Party Dish | Goes Great: Chilled | $\mathcal{S}$erve Mangiare |

*B*ruschetta

4 roma tomatoes, chopped

½ clove garlic, minced

1 tablespoon onions, chopped

1 teaspoon red wine vinegar or balsamic

2 tablespoons sweet basil, crushed

1 teaspoon olive oil

Salt and pepper

1 loaf Italian breads

½ cup parmesan cheese, grated

Toast the bread slices under broiler.

Clean the tomatoes and then cut into small cubes.

Then add all ingredients. Place on bread and add the parmesan cheese.

A fresh basil leaf is optional.

Mark and Rosalia
FAMILY FAVORITE

Serve Mangiare

*K*alamata Olive Bruschetta

¾ cup kalamata olives, pitted and chopped

½ clove garlic, minced

1 teaspoon olive oil

1 teaspoon red wine vinegar

2 tablespoons sun dried tomatoes in olive oil

A pinch of pepper

Mix all ingredients together. Place a spoonful on top of toasted Italian bread.

Sprinkle parmesan cheese on top.

Must try with
- Cheese
- Grapes
- Wine

Serve Mangiare

Chicago Style Pizza made Sicilian

1 package bread dough

2 cloves garlic, minced

2 tablespoons olive oil

Pizza sauce recipe in book

Pizza topppings, you name it; sky's the limit

Follow the directions on the bread dough label to rise.

Roll dough out on floured surface.

Transfer to 9x13 pan and rub garlic and a little olive oil all over the dough.

Put all the toppings on and put in a warm place

for about 20 min while your oven is preheating to 475. Bake for about 25 minutes.

Let stand for 5 minutes before cutting.

Any toppings can be used. My grandfather used Italian sausage in big chunks and cut up meat balls.

Serves:
6-8

Years ago, served at all family gathering

My grandfather was well known for his pizza, he would put sweet spaghetti sauce on his pizza.

Serve Mangiare

ROSALIE SCHWAMB

*B*ruschetta with *B*lood *R*ed *T*omatoes

Italian bread in slices
olive oil
sliced blood tomatoes
sliced Mozzarella cheese

Loaf Italian bread in slices

Drizzle with olive oil

Place sliced blood tomatoes (or any kind) on bread slices.

Slice Mozzarella cheese and place on tomatoes
and place basil leaves in between,
drizzle with a little more olive
oil and salt and pepper.

Crowd pleaser, great with some wine and fruit.

Serve
Mangiare

Zucchini Rolls

½ cup butter

1 cup light brown sugar

2 eggs

1 tablespoon orange juice

2 ½ cups flour

2 teaspoons baking powder

½ cinnamon

¼ teaspoon salt

1 ½ cups zucchini, shredded

Preheat oven to 350.

In bowl, mix the first 4 ingredients.

Mix in the combined next 4 ingredients.

Stir in the zucchini.

Drop by teaspoons onto a greased cookie sheet.

Bake about 10-12 minutes.

My Mother and I came up with this recipe while sitting up at the lake cabin.

Tales From the Kitchen:

This is a twist on my Grandmother's zucchini bread recipe. I always am trying to think of food that stores and travels well is tasty and good for you as well.

Serve Mangiare

ROSALIE SCHWAMB

Dressing & Salads

Sicilian Red

⅓ cup non fat yougart

2 tablespoons mayonnaise

2 tablespoons ketchup

2 teaspoons vinegar

Mix and pour over any greens

Great served with any meat dish.

Serve
Mangiare

ROSALIE SCHWAMB

*F*resh dressing for any green salad with vegetables

1 clove garlic minced
Salt and pepper
1 teaspoon dill weed

1 teaspoon Italian parsley
1 tablespoon lemon juice
½ cup yogurt plain.

Mix everything together and it's ready to eat

Classic Party Dish

Serve Mangiare

*B*alsamic Vinaigrette

1 clove garlic minced

1 teaspoon of Italian herbs

Salt and pepper

¼ cup of white or red Balsamic vinegar

1 cup olive oil

Put in medium deep mixing bowl.

Add Balsamic vinegar, garlic, herbs, salt, and pepper.

Whisk in olive oil.

Serve over any greens or vegetables

Serve
Mangiare

ROSALIE SCHWAMB

$\mathcal{F}$resh Lemon Vinaigrette

1 clove garlic minced

1 teaspoon of Italian herbs

Salt and pepper

Juice from 1 lemon

1 cup olive oil

Put garlic, herbs, salt, and pepper in medium deep mixing bowl.

Add juice from lemon.

Whisk in olive oil.

Serve over any greens or vegetables

This is one of the freshest vinaigrettes of all time.

Also great over bow tie pasta as a side dish.

Serve Mangiare

*T*omato and Cucumber Insalata

6 large roma tomatoes, ripe and sliced into wedges

2 cucumbers, cut into slices

1 red onion, thinly sliced

6 ounces pecorino cheese, coarsly grated

2 tablespoons fresh basil, shredded

1 teaspoon fresh oregano, chopped

Vinaigrette

⅓ cup olive oil

4 tablespoons balsamic vinegar; prefer white, can use red

½ teaspoon sugar

½ teaspoon salt

¼ teaspoon pepper

In large bowl combine tomato wedges, cucumbers, onions.

In small bowl, whisk together olive oil, vinegar, sugar, salt, pepper, and herbs. Pour over the tomato mixture. Add 2 teaspoons of water and toss.

Put into serving bowl and place the mixture on the oregano, basil, and grated cheese.

Serves: 4-6

Can be a cucumber salad or tomato salad. In this case, I combined them both.

Home FAMILY FAVORITE

Serve Mangiare

ROSALIE SCHWAMB

Cucumber Insalata

2 cucumbers, cut into slices

3 tablespoons white wine vinegar

1 tablespoon sugar

Salt & pepper

1 small red onions, sliced into rings

3 tablespoons fresh dill, chopped if you like

Wash the cucumbers and partially remove the peel in lengthwise strips using a vegetable peeler or fork, leaving a little skin between each strip.

Thinly slice the cucumber widthwise.

Place the vinegar, sugar, salt, and pepper in a bowl and whisk until the sugar is dissolved.

Add the cucumber, onion, and dill, and toss well.

The salad can be served at once, but it will improve in flavor if you let the ingredients marinate for 30 minutes.

Serves:

3-4

My husband Mark's favorite for anytime, but a must on holidays.

Serve Mangiare

*S*alad of all Salads

1 lb of any kind of pasta shapes.

½ cup of cherry tomatoes

1 lg cucumber, peeled and chopped

½ green pepper, chopped

½ red pepper, chopped

1 cup celery

1 cup green olives

½ cup of pepperoncini

¼ cup onion, chopped

4 oz salami, cut into strips

1 cup any kind of cheese, cubed

3 tablespoons olive oil

Lemon juice from 1 lemon

½ teaspoon dried Italian herbs

2 cloves of garlic, minced

¼ teaspoon mustard

Cook pasta as on the direction of the package until al dente.

Drain and put 1 tbsp of olive oil all over to keep from sticking.

Mix cherry tomatoes, cucumber, green pepper, red pepper, celery, green olives, pepperoncini, onion, salami, and cheese together in a large bowl with the pasta.

In small bowl, combine olive oil, lemon juice, dried Italian herbs, garlic, mustard, salt and pepper.

Whisk and pour over the all the ingredients mixed already.

My family is crazy about this pasta salad. I have to make it once a week.

Classic Party Dish

Goes Great:
AS LEFTOVERS

Serve Mangiare

ROSALIE SCHWAMB

$\mathcal{W}$arm Bread Insalata

2 lbs tomatoes cut into pieces

2 smalls zucchini peeled and cut into pieces

3 tablespoons olive oil

2 cups dried bread cubes

1 tablespoon garlic minced

2 tablespoons sugar

Salt and pepper

½ cup basil cut into pieces

1 cup Parmesan cheese

In saute pan, saute olive oil and bread cubes until brown.

In 9x13 pan, put in tomatoes, zucchini, garlic, sugar, salt, and pepper.

Cover with all the oil and add the bread, mix all.

Top with basil and parmesan cheese. Bake at 350 for 35 min.

Serves: 4-6

Cousin Ron's
FAMILY FAVORITE

$\mathcal{S}$erve
$\mathcal{M}$angiare

ROSALIE SCHWAMB

Warm Vegetable Insalata

1 pound red potatoes cubbed

8 oz asparagus spears cut into pieces

1 cup cherry tomatoes

6 cups arugula or anykind of greens

3 slices prosciutto (can also use salami)

½ cup shreaded Cheese Asiago or Parma Regiano

Vinaigrette

¼ cup olive oil

¼ cup white wine

2 tablespoons red onions finely chopped

2 tablespoons fresh herbs

1 lrg garlic, minced

½ teaspoon mustard (preferred brown)

Salt & pepper

Preheat oven to 425.

Place potatoes in a 13x9 pan. Toss in the vinaigrette. Roast potatoes for 20 min, tossing halfway.

Add the asparagus, tomatoes and more vinaigrette and bake 10 more min.

Serve on the greens and put the prosciutto and cheese.

Can also be served as a side dish—omit the greens.

Fresh and Easy to Make

Can be a dinner alone or a side dish if you leave out the greens.

Serve Mangiare

Bean Insalata

2 cans cannellini beans, drained

1 lrg onions, chopped

1 stalk celery

1 cucumber, chopped

5 cherry tomatoes, quartered

¼ cup olives, chopped

3 leaves sage, minced

1 clove garlic, minced

Salt and pepper

¼ cup olive oil

3 tablespoons lemon juice or you can use red wine vinegar

Olives are optional—any kind, about ¾ cup if you like to add to the recipe.

In large bowl combine beans, onions, celery, cucumber, tomatoes, sage, garlic, salt and pepper.

Add the olive oil and lemon juice, then stir gently and put into fridge for 1 hour.

Can be served as side dish over bread or as a bruchetta.

Serves: 4-6

My Nanu's
FAMILY FAVORITE

Serve Mangiare

ROSALIE SCHWAMB

Soups

L entil Soup (Lenticchie)

1 ½ cups of lentils

¼ cup olive oil

1 onion, chopped

¾ cup carrots, chopped

3 stalks celery, chopped

1 28-oz can tomatoes with liquid

½ cup Acini di pepe pasta

Place lentils in bowl of water and let soak overnight.

Drain and wash the lentils in warm water.

Place in 2 quarts pot of water and boil.

Add the oil, onion, celery and tomatoes in the boiling water.

Lower the heat to simmer and cook for 30 minutes. Add the acini di pepe pasta ,
cook for another 15 minutes.

Drizzle a bit of olive oil when serving.

One of my grandfather's favorite soups and boy, was he a soup lover. He would always grate a little Parmesan cheese over all soups. Tales From the Kitchen!

Serves:
4-6

Serve Mangiare

ROSALIE SCHWAMB

Pastina in Brodo

1 ½ lbs of soup meat and a good sized beef bone

1 onion chopped

½ cup celery, chopped

½ cup carrot, chopped

2 tablespoons parsley

½ lb of small pasta shells

Salt and pepper

Cook meat in 2 quarts of water. When cooked pull apart the meat.
Add rest of ingredients.
Cook until pasta is done.
Serve with some parmesan on top and Italian bread of course!

My Great Nana Rosa and Nanu Jerome,
they loved to dance and cook together.

Serve Mangiare

Sicilian Stew

3 pounds beef stew meat, cut, salt and peppered

3 cups good red wine, any kind you would drink

3 cloves garlic, mashed but not chopped

1 cup flour

1 tablespoon of salt

½ tablespoon of pepper

3 springs rosemary

1 onion, chopped big

3 carrots, chopped big

3 sticks celery, chopped big

1 bag small red potatoes, chopped big

2 cloves garlic, chopped fine

3 bay leaves

1 tablespoon italian herbs

1 cup vegetable stock

Put the stew meat in a bowl with the wine, garlic and rosemary. Let sit for 2 hours.

In the mean time, cut the onion, celery, carrots, and potatoes into about same size pieces.

Drain the beef but reserve the wine.

Put oven on 300.

Roll the beef in the flour mixture with the salt and pepper.

In saute pan, sire the beef and put into oven safe large crock pot.

Then in same saute pan, brown all the onions, celery and carrots and potatoes.

Put on the chopped garlic and italian herbs then put into the crock pot with the beef.

Add the wine to the saute pan and cook for a minute with the 1 cup of chicken or beef stock. Pour over the beef and vegetables and put in the bay leaves and the sprigs of rosemary from the wine.

Cook for 2 hours covered, serve with any red wine you would like, a deep burgundy is great.

Great with just a big hunk of Italian bread and butter.

Serves:
4-6

Always need a big hunk of Italian bread with stew.

Serve Mangiare

ROSALIE SCHWAMB

$\mathcal{B}$eef Vegetable Soup

6 cups beef broth

1 teaspoon basil, dried & crushed

4 potatoes, cubed

3 med carrots, chopped

3 stalks celery, chopped

1 lg onions, chopped (any kind)

1 can cannellini beans, drained

1 pound beef cooked and cut in bite size pieces (any kind)

Salt & pepper

1 tablespoon Worcestershire sauce

2 cups pasta, very small (acini de pepe or alphabet)

1 teaspoon olive oil

Stir the broth, basil, potatoes, carrots, celery, and onion in a 4-quart saucepan.

Over medium-high heat, heat to a boil.

Stir the beans, cooked beef, salt, pepper, worcestershire sauce, and olive oil in the saucepan.

Reduce the heat to low for 15 min, then add the pasta and simmer till done serve.

Serves:
4-6

*Serve
Mangiare*

Chicken Soup

3 chicken breasts

8 cups water

3 carrots cut into pieces

3 stalks celery, cut into pieces

4 large potatoes, peeled and cut into pieces

1 large onion, cut into pieces

Salt and pepper

½ lb pasta shells

2 packages seasoning broth, any seasoning brand

Put water in pot and add chicken. Cook until tender, about 20 min.

Then take chicken out of pot and let cool.

Add into pot the vegtables, salt, pepper and the seasoning.

Cook for 15 min then add the pasta. Cook until tender then add the chicken.

Papa Schwamb's wonderful chicken soup. Can't beat it. My husband always says if you sell this, you can make a fortune.

I make this when anyone has a cold--it has that curing effect.

Serve Mangiare

Virginia LaVora Woelky is my Auntie Jalina. She can put a smile on anyone's face. Her uplifting way of the world is right on. She is a florist by trade and a comedian by heart.

She has a great family, my uncle Howard, who is her husband, and their children, daughter Lucy, who is my cousin, and Lucy's husband Dan. Their children Jennifer, husband Dan, children Amelia, Andrea and Alecia, and son Tom. Her son Richard and his daughter's Kayla and Allison.

Here is auntie Jalina in her home making one of my family's favorite dishes.

$\mathcal{M}$inestrone

1 cup of celery chopped

2 carrots, diced

1 can of peas

1 large onion

3 medium potatoes, diced

½ cup olive oil

¾ cup tomato paste

¾ cup vermicelli

5 ½ quarts of water

1 tablespoon of sea salt

½ teaspoon pepper

Heat olive oil in pan. Add onions and potatoes and brown.

Add tomato paste, cook over low heat. Add the salt and pepper.

Boil 5 ½ quarts of water in a pot then add the celery and carrots and cook until tender.

Then add peas and vermicelli and when almost cooked add the potatoes and onions and tomatoes. Simmer for about 20 minutes.

Serve with parmesan cheese and tad bit of olive oil over the cheese and a big hunk of Italian bread.

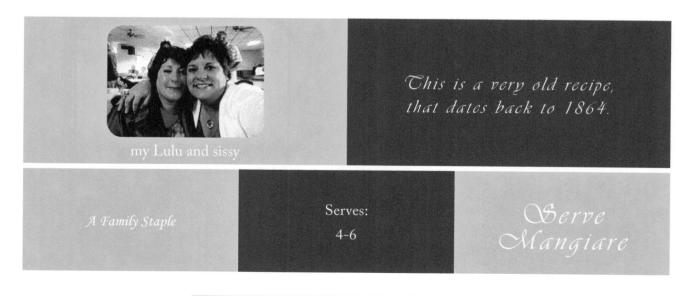

my Lulu and sissy

This is a very old recipe, that dates back to 1864.

A Family Staple

Serves:
4-6

Serve Mangiare

ROSALIE SCHWAMB

Cipolla (Onion Soup)

5 yellow onions, thinly sliced

3 tablespoons butter

3 tablespoons flour

½ cup bourbon whiskey

2 quarts beef broth

¼ teaspoon basil

Salt and pepper

8 slices Italian bread, toasted

1 cup grated swiss cheese

In a dutch oven, saute sliced onions in butter until soft.

Stir in flour to form a paste; pour in bourbon little by little, stirring until smooth. Add salt and pepper.

Gradually stir in broth; season with basil and simmer 30-40 minutes.

Drop a slice of toasted French bread into bottom of each soup bowl, fill with onion soup and sprinkle with cheese. Broil until cheese is golden and bubbly.

Serve immediately.

My honey and baby girl

Husband Mark's
Family Favorite

Serve Mangiare

Panini

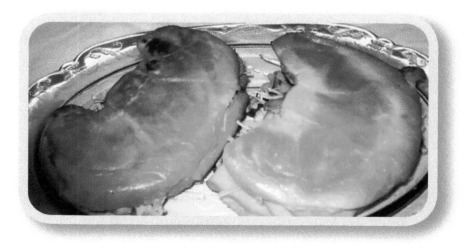

Croissant Panini

*In place of Ham, Salomi or anykind of sliced meat can be used

*In place of the Guda, any cheese can be used.

12 slices ham

2 cups arugula

8 slices guda cheese

2 tablespoons butter

4 croissants

Butter the croissants. Place 3 slices of ham, arugula, and 2 slices of cheese on each croissant.

Press on panini press or with 2 skillets till brown (if using the skillet, turn once brown).

Serves:
4-6

Great, easy, and fast to make when you want to watch a good movie. Maybe serve with some chips.

Serve Mangiare

Chicken Panini

Ciabatta bread or anykind of bread can be used

1 tablespoon pesto

1 grilled chicken breast

2 slices swiss gruyére cheese

2 slices prosciutto

2 larges Romaine lettuce leaves

Spread outside of both sides of the bread with a little butter.

Press and cook until golden. Serve and enjoy!

In place of the pesto you can use ranch dressing; very good.

My daughter and her Ranch dressing.

Serve Mangiare

M eat Panini

2 tablespoons Dijon style mustard

2 slices sourdough bread or you can use anykind of bread or roll

4 slices gruyére cheese

4 slices roast beef

¼ slice onions in rings

Spread both slices of bread with mustard and alternate with the beef and the cheese.

Spread outside of both sides of the bread with a little butter.

Press and cook until golden. Serve and enjoy!

Any kind of meat can be used.

Serve Mangiare

Mediterrean Panini

2 slices pork tenderloin, cooked

2 slices mozzarella cheese

2 tomatoe slices

4 basil leaves

1 teaspoon Italian herbs

Salt and pepper

2 slices Italian bread

Spread bread with olive oil. Sprinkle salt and pepper and herbs on both slices,
then layer with the rest of the ingredients.

Spread outside of both sides of the bread with a little butter.

Press and cook until golden. Serve and enjoy!

My mother was the sandwich queen.

Mama's favorite. You can use any cold cuts in place of the pork and drizzle a little olive oil and balsamic vinegar on top.

Serve Mangiare

Rosalie Schwamb

Family!

This is my husband Mark, my bear forever.

These are my children. Mark II, my prince, will do anything for anyone. If you are in need, all I have to do is call and he'll be there. I thank God everyday he was born.

Rosalia is my princess, not only is her beauty on the outside, but inside she can melt your heart. Her compassion for the elderly is truly wonderful. She is my blessing.

Chicken Florence

1 64-ounce bag chicken skinless

1 large onions sauteed

¼ cup butter

2 tablespoons paprika

1 tablespoon dry onion

1 teaspoon cayenne pepper

1 teaspoon garlic powder

1 teaspoon turmeric

1 teaspoon vinegar

1 teaspoon sugar

1 small carrots grated

¼ cup water

2 dashes pepper

1 cup evaporated milk

1 tablespoon cornstarch

1 pound egg noodles cooked see package

Preheat oven to 350.

Prepare all above ingredients in a big pan except water, pepper, milk and cornstarch. Saute for 15 min.

Put all into roaster and put in water. Cover with foil and cook for 30 min.

Take out of oven. Pour the drippings into a saute pan for 15 minutes.

In the saute pan with the drippings, put in 1 can evaporated milk. Mix with 1 tablespoon of cornstarch and pepper until smooth.

Pour over the chicken.

Zia Rosies recipe

Serves:
4-6

Orvieto

Serve Mangiare

Sicilian Saltimbocca

4 turkey fillets, cut in half to make 8 slices

½ cup fresh spinach

2 tablespoons of olive oil

1 onion, chopped

salt and pepper

2 slices prosciutto, cut in half to make 8 slices

¾ cup white wine

¾ cup chicken broth

8 fresh basil leaves

Pound turkey slices till flat. Add salt and pepper.

Place some spinach on turkey length wise.

Put a thin slice of prosciutto over the spinach length wise.

Place onion slices over the prosciutto, secure with a tooth pick and sire 3-4 minutes in pan with olive oil till brown, then add wine and chicken broth. Place basil leaves as well.

Simmer for 15-20 minutes until tender. Can be served with any of your favorate vegtables or rice.

Serves:
4-6

Comfort food for sure, serve with mashed potatoes.

Any Great Pinot

$Serve$
$Mangiare$

ROSALIE SCHWAMB

Stuffed Italian Turkey Breast

2 pounds turkey breast tenderloin

2 med zucchini, cut into small strips

2 carrots, cut into small strips

3 slices any kind of bread, cut into cubes

15 Italian olives, chopped

2 cloves garlic, chopped

5 tablespoons fresh basil, chopped

1 tablespoon mayonnaise

4 tablespoons Parmesan cheese

1 cup chicken broth

⅛ cup olive oil

2 tablespoons butter

Cut open the turkey in half, like a book.

Pound the meat to make larger.

Heat oven to 400.

Put the zucchini and carrots in a bowl of water and microwave for 2 min.

Drain the vegetables and place in bowl. Stir in the bread, olives, garlic, basil, parmesan cheese and mayo. Add salt and pepper.

Place the breast open and drizzle with olive oil, put all the ingredients on the breast and roll and tie up with string.

Heat the olive oil and butter in flame proof pan, brown, turn once.

Add the broth and cover. Bake for 15 min.

Take off cover and cook for 30 more min.

Serve with any white wine, full bodied Italian chardonnay.

my sweetness in yellow

all my cuginos

Italian chardonnay

Serve Mangiare

Chicken in White Sauce

2 pounds chicken, cubed

15 ounces chicken broth

1 cup onions, chopped

3 tablespoons brown mustard

2 tablespoons thyme, dried

1 teaspoon basil, dried

2 cloves garlic, chopped

1 cup sour cream

Salt

Pepper

Combine broth, onion, mustard, thyme, basil, and garlic, salt, and pepper in a pot.

Bring to a boil. Cover and simmer for 5 mintues. Lay chicken in pan. Cover and simmer for 15 minutes.

Remove chicken, bring liquid to a boil, uncovered, for 8 minutes.

Remove from heat, let cool slightly. Stir in sour cream, pour over chicken.

Very easy to make

Great with just a green salad

White Reisling

Serves: 4-6

Serve Mangiare

ROSALIE SCHWAMB

Cashew Chicken

2 egg whites

½ cup cornstarch

1 ½ pounds chicken breasts, cut in bite size pieces

6 tablespoons olive oil

2 tablespoons ginger root, minced

1 tablespoon white wine

2 tablespoons sugar

½ cup cashew nuts, chopped

3 tablespoons soy sauce

1 cup chicken broth

1 tablespoon cornstarch

1 6-oz pea pod

2 cups cooked rice

Place egg whites, beaten slightly, in shallow bowl.

Place ½ cup of cornstarch in another shallow bowl.

Dip the chicken pieces in egg whites then coat in cornstarch.

In skillet, heat the olive oil and add the ginger and chicken fry until chicken changes colors.

Add the wine, sugar, cashews and soy sauce.

Combine the chicken broth with the 1 tbsp of cornstarch then pour into the chicken mixture.

Add the pea pods, cover and simmer for 10 minutes.

Make the rice. When rice is done, chicken will be done. Put the chicken over the rice.

Passed Down From: My Mom's Kitchen
Serves: 4-6

When my mom made this, I said mom this isn't Italian, she said I made it so it is Italian.

Husband Mark's Family Favorite

Dry white or a Zinfindal

Serve Mangiare

Chicken and Rice in Wine Sauce

3 pounds chicken breasts or thighs cut in half

3 cups white wine

2 cups flour

Salt and pepper

2 cups rice pilaf or any kind you like all cooked

¼ cup olive oil

1 tablespoon butter

1 red bell pepper chopped

1 large onions chopped

2 cloves garlic minced

Cut the chicken in half and place in bowl with 2 cup of the wine and marinate.

Make the rice and set aside.

Take the chicken out of wine one at a time and dredge in flour salt and pepper.

Put chicken into skillet on medium with 2 tablespoons of butter and olive oil and cook until light brown.

Take out of skillet. In the same skillet, put in the peppers, onion and garlic and cook until almost tender.

Place the chicken on top of the the peppers and onions. Add 2 tablespoons of flour and stir.

Add the last cup of wine and simmer for about 20 min.

Place the rice around the sides. Garnish with parsley.

Any good white wine

Serve Mangiare

Rosalie Schwamb

$\mathcal{B}$ readed Chicken Breast

6 chicken breasts

1 ½ cups dry Italian bread crumbs

1 tablespoon italian herbs

⅛ cup Parmesan cheese

2 eggs

2 tablespoons milk or heavy cream

¼ cup olive oil

3 tablespoons butter

Mix bread crumbs, herbs, and cheese in shallow bowl

In another bowl, whisk together 2 eggs and milk.

One at a time, put the chicken in the egg and milk mixture then the bread crumb mixture.

When all chicken is breaded, put into a skillet on med-high with the oil and butter and fry until lightly brown on each side.

Add more oil as needed.

Can also cut into stripes after cooking and placed on top of spaghetti dinner. I have also placed on salad.

Serves:
4-6

Serve Mangiare

Chicken Tetrazzini

2 tablespoons butter

1 onion, chopped

2 cups mushrooms, sliced

2 tablespoons lemon juice

¼ teaspoon grated nutmeg

1 10 ¾-ounce can cream of mushroom soup

1 10 ¾-ounce can cheddar cheese soup

2 soup cans of half-and-half

1 cup mozzarella cheese, grated

¼ cup chicken broth

1 pound pasta any medium pasta, cooked al dente

4 cups cooked chicken = a 3 pound package of breasts

In large sauce pan, melt the butter. Saute the onions until tender then add the mushrooms and lemon juice. Cook for 3 minutes.

Season with salt, pepper and nutmeg.

Stir in broth, soups and half-and-half, then add the cheese and stir until cheese melts.

Take off heat.

In 3-quart buttered baking dish, put in half of the pasta, then all of the chicken, and then the rest of the pasta.

Spread the sauce all over and inbetween the pasta and the chicken.

Bake uncovered on 375 for 30 to 40 minutes.

Serves:
4-6

Serve Mangiare

ROSALIE SCHWAMB

Wrapped Chicken Italian Style

4 chicken breasts skinned and cut horizontally along the length to form a pocket

4 ounces creamy havarti cheese, sliced (or you can use any cheese variation you like)

2 cloves garlic, minced

1 tablespoon italian herbs

8 slices prosciutto

2/3 cup red wine

2/3 cup chicken broth

1 teaspoon brown sugar

Take the chicken open like a pocket on all four and salt and pepper.

Sprinkle the garlic and herbs.

Stuff with a slice of cheese.

Close the chicken pockets and wrap the prosciutto over the chicken.

Secure with string or tooth picks.

Pour the wine and the chicken broth into frying pan and bring to a boil.

When it just starts to boil, add the brown sugar.

Stir to resolve.

Put the heat to simmer and place the chicken in the pan for 15 minutes.

Remove chicken from the pan right away and cover with foil to keep warm

Reheat the sauce to a boil then put heat to low until thickened.

Remove the toothpicks or string and place the chicken in a serving dish. Cut into slices and pour the sauce over the chicken.

Serves:
4-6

Dry white or a Zinfindal

Serve
Mangiare

Chicken Parmesan

1 cup of Italian bread crumbs

½ cup Parmesan cheese

1 tablespoon Italian herbs

1 egg

12 chicken tenders

⅛ cup olive oil

1 cup of shredded cheese Mozzarella

1 cup of Marinara sauce (use jar or make one of my sauce recipes)

Heat oven to 375

Beat eggs in bowl.

Mix bread crumbs, parmesan cheese and Italian herbs in bowl.

Bread the chicken in the egg then the bread crumb mixture.

In sauté pan, put the olive oil and butter on med high.

Sauté the chicken 3 min on each side then place in 13x9 baking dish.

Spoon over the marinara sauce and sprinkle the cheese.

Bake for 15 minutes or until bubbly.

Serve with a green salad or any pasta dish.

My son Mark's Family Favorite

Serves: 4-6

Serve Mangiare

Tuscany Chicken Rollups

6 chicken breasts, pounded out

⅛ cup olive oil

Salt and pepper

4 sprigs thyme

6 strips prosciutto

6 slices mozzarella cheese

1 15 ½-ounce jar fire roasted red peppers

6 sweet basil leaves

12 asparagus spears

¼ cup olive oil

1 tablespoon butter

2 cups marinara sauce (jar or you can try my homemade)

Preheat oven to 350.

Assemble all at one time.

Take pounded out chicken breast and place all on board.

Spread some olive oil on chicken breast. Add salt, pepper and the springs of thyme. Sprinkle the leaves on all the chicken.

Place a whole roasted pepper on the chicken then the prosciutto and cheese.

Place 2 asparagus and one basil leaf on each one.

Roll them carefully together and place some tooth picks to hold.

In saute pan, pan stir the chicken in olive oil and a tab butter until brown on all sides.

When done, place in 8x8 roasting pan and pour the marinara sauce on and bake for 40 min.

Serves: 4-6

Served great with salad or pasta with a little lemon, olive oil, and fresh herbs salt and pepper.

Any good white or red wine

Fancy but Easy

Serve Mangiare

Seafood

Shrimp Scampi

1 lb. of pasta, any kind, cooked al dente

12 large shrimp, cleaned and deveined

2 tablespoons of flour

Salt and pepper

3 tablespoons olive oil

1 tablespoon butter

2 cloves garlic, minced

2 tablespoons fresh basil, chopped

3 tablespoons lemon juice

In shallow bowl, place the flour, salt, and pepper.

Add the shrimp.

Dust them off and place in sauté pan on med heat. Add the olive oil and butter.

Add the garlic. Cook for 2 minutes on both sides.

Take off heat and add the basil.

Stir in the pasta and serve with parmesan cheese.

My mama and I loved to make this dish for family gatherings.

Serves: 4-6

A salad and white Zinfandel wine

Serve Mangiare

Salmon Pesto

4 fillets salmon

Juice from 1 lemon

Salt and pepper

Olive oil

Pesto prepared

Salt and pepper salmon fillets on both sides. Pour a small amount of olive oil on fillets and grill in oven at 375 degrees until tender and knife runs through smooth.

Spread each fillet with pesto.

Serves: 2-4

Great served with gnouche or any cooked pasta.

white Zinfandel

3 minutes on each side

Serve Mangiare

ROSALIE SCHWAMB

Fish with Rice (Pesci con Rice)

2 cups chicken broth

1 cup mixed vegetables

1 cup celery, chopped

1 clove garlic, chopped

1 tablespoon italian seasoning, dried

1 ¾ cups rice, uncooked brown or white

1 pound white fish or any kind you like

In skillet combine broth, vegetables, and celery.

Bring to boil and then reduce the heat to medium.

Cover and cook for 3 minutes.

Uncover, return to a boil, and stir in the rice.

Top with the fish, garlic, salt, pepper, and italian seasoning.

Reduce heat and cover for 12 minutes or until fish is flaky.

Serves:
2-4

Dry white wine, Verdicchio

Serve Mangiare

Scallops with Asparagus

5 red potatoes, cut into slices

1 pound asparagus spears, cut in half

15 scallops

6 cups Romaine lettuce, cut into pieces

1 tablespoon apple cider vinegar

1 teaspoon grain mustard

1 small red onions, minced (reserve some for garnish)

4 tablespoons olive oil

Place Romaine in serving dish.

Mix the last 4 ingredients in bowl and whisk. Set aside.

Boil pot of water. Add salt and sliced potatoes. Cook for 4 minutes.

Drain potatoes and place in skillet with asparagus and 3 tablespoons of butter.

Saute for 5 minutes then, in same skillet, move the potatoes and asparagus to one side.

Place the scallops on the other side with 2 more tablespoons of butter and saute for 2 minutes on both sides.

Put all the cooked ingredients on the romaine and pour the dressing on top and garnish with red onion.

Serves: 4-6

White Pinot

My soul sister Kelly loved this dish.

Serve Mangiare

ROSALIE SCHWAMB

Fettichini Alfredo with Seafood

12 oz frozen Shrimp, peeled and deveined

1 ½ cups any veggies, cooked and drain

8 oz pasta, any kind, preferred rotini

¼ cup butter

1 cup heavy cream

1 clove garlic, crushed

1 ½ cups finely grated Parmesan cheese

Boil water in large sauce pan. Put in the pasta for 8-10 minutes.

Add the shrimp and cook for another 3 minutes.

Drain and return back to the pan, put in the veggies.

Melt butter in a medium saucepan over medium low heat. Add cream and simmer for 5 minutes, then add garlic and cheese and whisk quickly, heating through.

Pour over the pasta and veggies.

Serves:
4-6

Great with:
Lobster tail cut up in this pasta or shrimp

Serve Mangiare

$\mathcal{H}$erb Seafood Southern Sicily

1 head Romaine lettuce, the leaves laid down on serving dish

20 scallops

20 shrimp, large ones or prawns, cooked, peeled, and drained

4 tablespoons vinegar

3 tablespoons orange juice

4 tablespoons lime juice

1 clove garlic, minced

¼ green bell pepper, cut into slices

2 ounces green olives, sliced in half

2 tablespoons cilantro, chopped

½ cup olive oil

Place scallops in sauce pan with just enough water to cover.

Bring to simmer for 2 minutes, cool. When cooled, place scallops and shrimps in a bowl and add the vinegar, lime, orange juice and garlic. Mix well then cover for 1 ½ hours.

Strain seafood mixture, reserving the marinade. In a salad bowl, place the seafood, peppers, olives and cilantro.

Toss the olive oil into the reserved marinade, pour over the salad and serve.

Serves:
6-8

Serve Mangiare

ROSALIE SCHWAMB

Crab Fritada

3 smalls zucchini grated

1 cup crab meat

2 tablespoons red onions grated

2 eggs

6 to 8 tablespoons flour

1 teaspoon baking powder

1 teaspoon salt

½ teaspoon pepper

Mix all ingredients above in saute pan. Add in 1 to 2 tablespoons of butter and some olive oil.

Fry for 2 minutes on each side.

This is great cold for picnics or parties, can make ahead and store in foil in fridge.

Serve Mangiare

Ocean Trout on Pasta Bed

2 tablespoons olive oil

12 spring onions, chopped

¼ cup sugar

3 ounces fish sauce

3 ounces fresh ginger, minced

8 chillies, chopped

2 tablespoons lime juice

8 ounces spaghetti, cooked and drained with a little olive oil mixed

1 bunch cilantro, chopped

1 pound ocean trout fillets, cut into large pieces

Heat oil in saute pan and saute the onions until golden.

Add the sugar and dissolve. Cook on med heat for 4 minutes until mixture has carmelized.

Stir well. Add the fish sauce, ginger, chilies and lime juice.

Stir well. Remove from heat and cover.

Place the cooked pasta in a bowl and put in the cilantro and some of the sugar mixture just to moisten the pasta.

Pan fry or grill the fish fillets about 2 minutes on each side, let cool and arrange on the pasta. Spoon the sauce over the fillets and serve.

This has been passed down from my Auntie Jalina.

Serves:
4-6

Serve Mangiare

ROSALIE SCHWAMB

Tuscan Fish

¼ cup olive oil

1 cloves garlic, minced

½ teaspoon dried Italian herbs

½ teaspoon rosemary

2 tablespoons balsamic vinegar (red or white)

Salt and pepper

2 lbs. of trout, perch or cod

In bowl, combine all ingredients except the fish. After mixed, set aside ¼ cup of the mixture then dredge the fish in the remaining mixture.

Grill or broil 2 minutes per side.

Put the fish on a plate and pour the reserved marinade.

Serve with White Zinfandel or Pinot Grigio.

This is great for grilling, love it for up at the cabin.

This is very inexpensive to make, put some rice around the dish or even pasta with one of my dressings.

Serve Mangiare

Shrimp Piccata

3 tablespoons of flour

1 teaspoon of fresh herbs

1 lb of shrimp, cleaned and devained
(you can keep shells on if you like)

3 tablespoons olive oil

2 cloves of garlic, finely chopped

1 tablespoon of capers

½ cup white wine

½ cup chicken stock

3 tablespoons of lemon juice

2 tablespoons of butter

3 cups of cooked seasoned rice or any kind you
would like

Toss shrimp together with the flour and herbs.

Heat oil on med high. Add the shrimp and cook
for 2 min and then turn.

Cook for another min then remove the shrimp.

In same pan, add the garlic, capers, wine, stock
lemon juice and butter.

Bring to a simmer and serve over the rice and
shrimp. Garnish with parsley.

Serves:
6-8

*My mama made this when I would
come over to her home and watch
the Food Network shows and eat.*

*Serve
Mangiare*

Rosalie Schwamb

Shrimp Scampi with Pasta and Asparagus

¼ lb Shrimp

8 spears of asparagas

2 Cloves Pressed Garlic

¼ tsp Salt

1 Tbsp Olive Oil

2 Tbsp Butter

1 Tbsp Chopped parsley

1 tsp Lemon Juice

Over medium heat melt the butter, olive oil and the garlic. Don't get the pan too hot. Or you'll burn the garlic. Put in the shrimp and any vegetable you would like. Turn heat to simmer on one side until they're done half way through and then turn them and cook till done. Add the Pasta and cheese if you would like.

Passed down from my Aunt MaryAnn's kitchen.

White Zinfandel

Serve Mangiare

Meat

Crusted Italian Beef

2 roasted bell peppers any kind pepper red, yellow or green roasted and cut in big slices

2 tablespoons olive oil

1 cup onions any kind, chopped

2 cloves garlic, minced

1 cup spinach fresh

2 to 3 lb round steak, pounded (or any kind of steak)

5 slices cheese, any kind, preferred provolone or mozzarella

Salt and pepper

¾ cup bread crumbs

2 tablespoons rosemary, chopped

3 tablespoons basil, chopped

3 tablespoons horseradish

3 tablespoons olive oil

Salt and pepper

Preheat oven to 400.

Heat the onions and garlic in sauce pan and 2 tab of olive oil until tender on med heat.

Gently pound the steak.

Line the steak with the peppers. On top of the peppers lay the onion mixture, the spinach, cheese, and salt and pepper. Roll the steak and secure with some twine or you could use heavy tooth picks. Place the beef on long roasting pan and brush olive oil on top.

For the crust that covers the top of the beef, mix together the bread crumbs, herbs and horseradish. Top the beef and press to make sure all of the beef is covered.

Serves: 4-6

Cooking time depends. If you like your meat rare to medium, cook 20-25 minutes.

Dry Red Aged, Taurino Notarpanaro Rosso del Salento

Serve Mangiare

Sicilian Pepper Steak

2 pounds round steak trim fat, cut across the grain into strips

½ cup soy sauce

2 cloves garlic, chopped

2 teaspoons ginger, grated

½ cup olive oil

1 tablespoon butter

1 ½ cups onions, chopped

1 ½ cups red bell peppers, chopped, can substitute green pepper

3 stalks celery, chopped

3 tomatoes, chopped

Combine soy sauce, garlic and ginger. Mix in beef.

Heat olive oil and butter on medium high, put in the beef and cook till brown and tender.

Add onions, peppers, and celery. Cook for 10 more minutes.

Then add tomatoes till heated through.

Serve over any type of pasta.

Serves:
4-6

Must Try with 1 lb of any Pasta

Merlot

Serve Mangiare

ROSALIE SCHWAMB

*R*agu of Beef

3 tablespoons olive oil

1 med onions, chopped

1 stalk celery, chopped

2 cloves garlic

1 lb beef ground beef

1-24 oz can crushed tomatoes

1 can tomato sauce

¼ cup red wine

1 tablespoon sweet basil

1 tablespoon oregano

Dash of nutmeg

Salt and pepper

Cook beef in pan until done and drain.

Set aside.

Heat oil in large sauce pan over medium heat and saute onion, celery and garlic.

Stir in meat and add tomatoes, sauce, wine, basil, oregano, a dash of nutmeg, salt, and pepper.

Simmer 1 hour, serve over any pasta, egg noodles, or rice.

My son Mark's Family Favorite

Serves: 6-8

Serve Mangiare

Sirloin with Pasta and Gravy

3 lbs beef sirloin steaks

Salt and pepper

2 tablespoons thyme

2 tablespoons butter

1 cup water

1 tablespoon olive oil

1 cup water

2 tablespoons cornstarch

3 tablespoons sour cream

1 lb cooked pasta, any kind, rigatoni preferred

Rub sirloin with salt, pepper, and thyme.

In saute pan, braise the sirloin in the butter and olive oil on medium heat. Cook for about 5 minutes.

Turn heat to low, pour in water and let simmer for 20 min.

Take off heat and cover the saute pan with foil and let sit for 20 min.

Take sirloin and cut against the grain into thin strips and then in half.

To make gravy: Take the drippings from the pan and heat. Take 2 tablespoons of cornstarch and 1 cup water, mix, then add to heated drippings and whisk until thick. Stir in 3 tablespoons of sour cream.

Put the sirloin in the pan and then toss in the pasta.

This is fast and easy and the kids will love the gravy; also wonderful overm ashed potatoes.

Serve Mangiare

ROSALIE SCHWAMB

Sicilian Beef Patties

1 pound ground beef

½ cup dry Italian bread crumbs

¼ cup Parmesan cheese, grated

1 teaspoon sweet basil dried

1 small onions, chopped

1 tablespoon water

¼ cup olive oil

1 tablespoon butter

1 egg

Mix together the beef, bread crumbs, cheese, basil, onions, egg and water.

In saute pan, put in the oil and butter on medium heat.

Brown both sides, 3-4 minutes on each side.

Turn heat to low and cook for 25 minutes.

Fast and easy, to loose some of the fat you can bake instead of fry.

Serve Mangiare

This is my Godmother Joanna with her famous meatloaf. Joanna LaVora Lemke, to me she is my Pena (godmother). She has been a big influence in my life. She is the most wonderful cook of all time. She is very kind and has the biggest heart ever. She has a great family, my uncle Tim who is Pena's husband and their children Son Jerome we call him Dune most handsome, (wife Marni who I adore and their children Joshua. Jordan and niece Rylee). Pena's daughter is Kelly, my wonderful soul sister. Her husband is Jack, you can't get much closer to heaven then him. Their children, son Jake, his wife Julie, son Cole, daughter Kathy, son Ashtyn, and daughter Lindsey, I call her Lynd's of all time life.

Here Pena is in her kitchen where she loves to spend a lot of her time. Pena is making her most famous meatloaf.

Sicilian Meatloaf

2 pounds ground beef

1 med onions, finely chopped

2 eggs

½ cup Parmesan cheese, grated

1 cup dry Italian bread crumbs

½ cup water

1 teaspoon sugar

Sm can italian tomatoes sauce

1 cup mozzarella cheese, shredded

Mix first seven ingredients and place in loaf pan.

Cover and bake at 350 for 1 hour and 45 minutes.

Take meat loaf out of pan and drain liquid. Put meat loaf back into pan and pour tomato sauce on top and then cover with mozzarella cheese.

Put back into oven and bake until sauce is bubbling and cheese melts, about 10-15 minutes. Let sit 5 minutes before you serve.

My godmother Joanna's recipe

Try this meatloaf recipe, it's my family's all time favorite!

Merlot

Serve Mangiare

Veal Parmigiano

In place of veal, you can use pork tenderloin cutlets or even chicken

¾ cup Parmesan cheese

1 teaspoon itialian seasoning

1 cup dry Italian bread crumbs

2 eggs

½ cup milk

2 pounds veal cutlets

1 tablespoon butter

½ cup olive oil

1 14.5 ounce can tomato sauce

1 cup mozzarella cheese, shredded

Preheat oven to 350.

In one shallow bowl, mix together the parmesan cheese, herbs and bread crumbs. In another shallow bowl, put the eggs and milk.

Pound veal out with meat mallet.

Dip the veal in the egg and milk mixture then dip into the breadcrumb mixture. Cover both sides.

Saute in hot olive oil and a tablespoon of butter, add more oil if needed, for about 2 minutes on med high heat, or until light golden brown.

When all cutlets are browned, put into a deep baking dish add the tomato sauce and top with the mozzarella cheese, bake uncovered until sauce is hot and cheese is melted, about 15 minutes.

Serves: 4

Great with any pasta, potato, or rice dish.

Chianti

Serve Mangiare

*B*readed Sicilian Steak

8 sandwhich steaks or any kind of thin steaks

1 ½ cups dry Italian bread crumbs

1 tablespoon sweet basil

⅛ cup Parmesan cheese

2 eggs

2 tablespoons milk or heavy cream

¼ cup olive oil

3 tablespoons butter

Mix in shallow bowl the bread crumbs, basil, and cheese

Mix in another bowl the 2 eggs and milk.

Whisk.

One at a time, dip the steaks in the egg and milk mixture then the bread crumb mixture.

When all beef is breaded, put into a skillet on med high heat with the oil and butter and fry until lightly brown on each side.

This was one of my Mama's all time dishes. She would make it for our family at least once a week.

Great with: any side salad, potatoes or pasta dish

Serve Mangiare

Lemon Herb Meatballs

1 lb ground beef

½ lb ground turkey

2 eggs

½ cup parmesan cheese

¾ cup dried bread crumbs

3 cloves of garlic, chopped

2 tablespoon minced parsley

1 tablespoon dried basil

¾ teaspoon dried oregano leaves

¾ teaspoon dried thyme leaves

1 lemon, grated and juiced

Salt and pepper

Mix all together and cook meatballs over med heat ¼ cup olive oil and 1 tab butter until browned on all sides

Cook for about 10-15 minutes.

Serves 6 and great with any pasta dish or salad.

Hint: if you make them small they dont take very long to cook, also great as a sandwich for later.

Serve Mangiare

Rosalie Schwamb

*I*talian Stuffed Peppers

1 lb ground beef, cooked

6 med peppers, any color

1 cup rice, cooked

4 tablespoons olive oil

1 large onions, chopped

2 cloves garlic, chopped

4 tablespoons red wine

3 tablespoons fresh parsley, chopped

½ cup mozzarella cheese, shredded

¼ cup Parmesan cheese

Salt and pepper

Preheat oven to 375.

In large frying pan, heat the oil and sauté the onions until soft.

Stir in the garlic. Add wine and cook for 5 minutes. Remove from the heat and add the meat, rice, parsley, mozzarella cheese, and parmesan cheese. Season well with salt and pepper.

Cut off the tops of the pepper, wash, and pat dry. Sprinkle with salt and pepper.

Stuff the peppers and top with the remaining 2 tablespoons of parmesan cheese and sprinkle with olive oil. Place in shallow baking dish. Fill the dish with a ½ inch of water.

Bake for 25 minutes.

I just serve this with salad.

Serve Mangiare

Grandma Eva's Beef Wraps "Pigs in the Blanket"

3 lb round steak, cut into 2 by 4 inch strips and pounded out.

Salt and pepper

1 lg onion, cut into medium chunks

½ package of bacon, cut the strip in half

Toothpicks

5 tablespoons of butter

2 ½ cups beef broth

Place steak down salted and peppered, put a piece of the bacon down and then the onion and wrap and secure with 2 tooth picks continue till all meat is done.

Sire the meat is frying pan on medium with just a tablespoon of butter to get all sides of the meat nice and brown then when meat is browned put in the rest of the butter and the beef broth. Simmer the meat for about 3-4 hours on low. covered. You can add mushrooms about 1 hour before serving this is optional.

When meat is fork tender you can reserve liquid to make a gravy to pour over any type of pasta or just use the dripping to serve over the meat.

Electric fry pan or slow cooker would work great.

This is my husbands grandmother Evelyn's recipe. She was the coolest grandma you would ever want to meet.

Serve Mangiare

ROSALIE SCHWAMB

Aunt MaryAnn with her famous Liver and Onions (sweet sour)

1 lb of Liver

1 cup of Italian bread crumbs

2 eggs

½ cup oil

2 tablespoons butter

2 onions sliced thinly

¾ cup water

¾ cup vinegar

¾ cup sugar

Slice the liver into long pieces.

Bread in egg and then bread crumbs.

Fry in saute pan with oil, 3-5 minutes per side.

Take out of pan and place in plate with foil to keep warm.

With the same saute pan, cook the onions in the butter until golden brown.

Add the water, vinegar and sugar. Cook until bubbly then pour over the liver.

MaryAnn LaVora Sentell, she is my Auntie. She is one of the best bakers I know. She is also a ribbon holder. She is a very strong lady fighting for her life with cancer. She has a great family, My uncle Corky who is her husband and their children and grandchildren, daughter Angie who is my sweetest cousin in my life, Jerome & Courtney who is our cuddle bug. Melissa, husband Chey and their children, Shelby, Maizzy and Duke.

Here is auntie MaryAnn in her kitchen making one of my family's favorite dishes.

One of my cousin Angie's favorite dishes. She is my sweetness.

Serve Mangiare

*I*talian Roast Beef

1 large beef sirloin steak or any type of beef roast

Salt and Pepper

3 cloves garlic minced

1 tablespoon italian herbs

3 tablespoons butter

1 large onions sliced big chucks

3 cups beef broth

2 tablespoons Worcestershire sauce

2 bay leaves

Turn slow cooker on med high.

Salt and pepper the beef on both sides. Poke holes into the beef and rub the garlic and herbs on the beef.

Place 1 tab of the butter and sire both sides of the beef till dark brown.

When all sired, add the rest of the butter.

Put the onion, 1 bay leaf, broth and worcestershire sauce on the beef.

Cook for 6 hours on low to med heat or until tender in cooker.

Cut and serve just as or can make the gravy with the drippings and serve with cheese in a bun.

This is great with egg noodles or shell pasta.

Sire the meat in a saute pan and then transfer to a slow cooker for the best results.

Gravy is easy to make, after you take the beef out of the slow cooker to cut take bay leaf out and put the cooker pan on the stove. Either 2 tablespoons of flour to make gravy or 2 tablespoons of cornstarch. if you make with cornstarch add 1 and ½ cup water & mix the 2 tablespoons of cornstarch then add to the pan while it is boiling stir then turn off and there is your gravy.

Serve Mangiare

*I*talian Sausage and Beans

8 sweet Italian sausages

1 lg onions, chopped

2 cloves garlic, chopped

1 green pepper, chopped

1 14-ounce can of tomatoes

2 tablespoons tomato paste (they have this in a tube for no waste)

1 14-ounce can cannellini beans, drained

1 tablespoon olive oil

Cook italian sausage for 10-15 minutes in boiler or pan fry. When done, put in dish and cover with foil.

Heat the oil in frying pan, add the onion, garlic and peppers. Cook 5 minutes.

Then add the tomatoes, stir in the tomatoe paste and beans. Cut the sausages and place in pan.

Cook on Medium heat for 5 minutes and serve.

My Nana Rosalie's recipe served with Bread of life.

This is an olden day recipe. All in one meal..Heaven

Galinano

Serve Mangiare

Pork

Pork Scaloppine

4 ounces portabella mushrooms cut into strips

2 red and green bell peppers, cut into strips

4 tablespoons butter

Salt and pepper

2 tablespoons olive oil

Heat oil and butter in skillet. Add the peppers and mushrooms. Cook until tender.

Add the salt and pepper.

Make the breaded pork chopped from this book

Make the marinara sauce from this book.

Place the breaded pork chops after cooked on plate then add the pepper and mushrooms and pour the marinara sauce on top.

This can also be made with chicken.

Serve Mangiare

Pork Tenderloin Stuffed

1 whole pork tenderloin, cut down middle

Salt and pepper

Olive oil

1 red bell pepper, chopped

¼ teaspoon thyme

¼ teaspoon rosemary

1 teaspoon basil

3 tablespoons Parmesan cheese

3 tablespoons horseradish mustard

2 cups white wine

1 ½ tablespoons flour

Preheat oven to 425.

Take pork tenderloin, cut down the middle, leaving enough room to stuff.

Salt and pepper the inside of the meat. Sprinkle the basil, red peppers, and parmesan cheese over the inside of the tenderloin. Add a little olive oil.

Fold the tenderloin back together and rub the horseradish mustard all over the top.

Salt and pepper and sprinkle the thyme and rosemary on it.

Pour olive oil on top and place into oven. After 25 min, pour white wine over the meat and add 3 tab flour.

Simmer for 10 minutes until reduced, then add a splash of milk and stir for a couple minutes.

Cut and pour the gravy over top and serve.

This is a wonderful dish to serve with just a green salad.

Great leftovers!

Add any vegetables you would like. I used carrots because they give a sweet taste. Just cook and slice and add to the inside of the pork

Serve Mangiare

Pork Chops with Balsamic and Shallots

2 tablespoons olive oil

1 tablespoon butter

1 lb pork chops, pounded
and cut into 1 inch pieces

Salt and pepper

2 cups shallots, chopped

1 clove garlic, chopped

½ cup water

2 tablespoons balsamic vinegar

Heat 1 tablespoon olive oil and butter in skillet on med high.

Salt and pepper the pork then cook in skillet until brown, or about 3 minutes on each side.

Put the pork in a serving dish and cover right away with foil to keep warm and finish cooking.

Add the last tablespoon of olive oil to the skillet. Cook the shallots for about 5 minutes then add the garlic.

Add the water and the balsamic vinegar, let simmer for 5 minutes. Stir in salt and pepper.

Pour over the pork. Serve.

This is a great dinner to serve with just a green salad and a baked potato.

Chardonnay

Serve Mangiare

Breaded Pork Chops Italian Style

6 pork chops pounded

1 ½ cups dry Italian bread crumbs

1 teaspoon basil

1 tablespoon parsley fresh chopped

2 tablespoons Parmesan cheese

2 eggs

2 tablespoons mik or heavy cream

¼ cup olive oil

3 tablespoons butter

Pound out the pork chops.

Mix in shallow bowl the bread crumbs, basil, parsley, and cheese.

Mix in another bowl the 2 eggs and milk.

Whisk.

One at a time, dip the chop in the egg and milk mixture then the bread crumb mixture.

When all pork is breaded, put into a skillet set on med high heat with the oil and butter and fry until lightly brown on each side.

Serve.

To make with sauce and peppers, take 2 large red or green peppers sliced and one onion, saute in pan for 15 minutes, pour in 2 cups of your favorite sauce, and serve over chops.

Serve Mangiare

*I*talian Stuffed Pork Chops

½ pound of med size mushrooms, any kind

½ cup onion, chopped

½ celery, chopped

½ cup (1 stick) of butter

1 cup bread crumbs

¼ teaspoon sage

½ cup chopped herbs, any kind

4-6 pork chops, double center and cut in the sides to make pocket.

Tooth picks

Salt and pepper

1 cup white wine or you can use chicken broth

In oven-proof large saute pan, saute sliced mushrooms, onions and celery in ½ cup of butter.

Cook for about 3 min on med then add the breadcrumbs, sage and herbs. Cook for 30 sec and then turn off heat. Take the pork chop, salt and pepper the inside and outside of each chop.

Stuff the chops with the mushroom mixture and secure with tooth picks.

In the same oven-proof saute pan, using the remaining butter, saute the chops until brown on both sides.

Pour the wine over, cover, and bake in oven at 350 degrees.

Bake for 1 hour and serve.

I found this recipe in my Nana's recipes. I made it, and it's wonderful, you will love it.

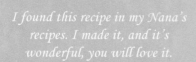

Serve Mangiare

Pastas

Spaghetti & Meatballs

1 egg

¾ cup Italian bread crumbs

¼ cup onion, chopped

¼ teaspoon of salt

¼ teaspoon of pepper

¼ teaspoon Italian seasoning

½ lb ground beef

½ lb ground pork

1 tbs olive oil

1 tbs Butter

1 lb of pasta Spaghetti

For the sauce, make any of the red sauces in this book.

Preheat oven to 375

Take the olive oil and butter and spread in a 9x13 baking pan.

Mix the first eight ingredients and roll into about 30 1-inch meatballs.

Put the meatballs in the baking dish and bake for about 20 minutes.

You already have your sauce, so now make your pasta and drain. Place the pasta in the dish with a little olive oil mixed in to keep from sticking.

When the meatballs are done, place on spaghetti.

Pour the sauce over the pasta and meatballs.

Every Sunday my Nana would make this wonderful dish.

Serve Mangiare

Pasta Salad

2 lbs pasta, any kind you like

1 stalk celery, chopped

1 green pepper, chopped

1 red bell pepper, chopped

1 yellow bell pepper, chopped

1 head cauliflower, chopped

1 head broccoli, chopped

1 cup green olives or any other kind

1 cup tomatoes (cherry preferred)

1 cup salami, cut in pieces

3 cups cheese, cubbed, any kind you like

1 tablespoon italian herbs

1 tablespoon old bay seasoning

2 gloves garlic, minced

Salt and pepper to taste and thyme

1 cup olive oil

½ cup balsamic vinegar, any kind you like

Put all ingredients, minus the seasonings, in a large bowl.

In separate bowl, combine old bay seasoning, garlic, salt, pepper, thyme and Italian herbs.

Then put in the balsamic vinegar and slowly whisk in the olive oil.

Pour the seasoning mixture over all the other ingredients and let marinate in the fridge for 1 hour.

Serves alot. Great leftovers for the week, just keep tightly sealed.

Cauliflower and broccoli are optional. Can use Pepperonis's just place in and also ham in place of the salami.

Serve Mangiare

ROSALIE SCHWAMB

Pasta Pesto and Turkey

3 cups pasta, any kind, bow tie preferred

2 cups cooked turkey, cubed (can also use chicken)

½ cup pesto (can use pesto recipe in book)

½ cup roasted peppers, chopped

¼ cup Parmesan cheese

Cook pasta, drain, and put back in pan.

Add cooked turkey, pesto, and roasted peppers. Mix well.

Place on serving plate and sprinkle cheese on top.

You may want to add more pesto if you want more pungent.

Serve
Mangiare

Linguini with Pesto and Green Beans

½ lb green beans (can also use peas and carrots)

8 ounces liguini cooked al dente

¼ cup pesto

½ cup sun dried tomatoes, in olive oil, sliced or roasted red pepper

Salt and pepper

½ cup Parmesan cheese or Asiago cheese

Boil water and cook the green beans 8 to 10 minutes, drain and pat dry.

Toss the cooked pasta with pesto, green beans and sun dried tomatoes. Sprinkle in salt, pepper, and cheese.

Serve
Mangiare

Rigatoni with Salsiccia

2 tablespoons olive oil

5 cloves garlic, minced

1 small onions, chopped finely

1 tablespoon mixed italian herbs

1 12-ounce can tomato paste

1 14.5 ounce can diced tomatoes

1 29-ounce can tomato sauce

1 cup water

Salt and pepper

⅛ cup sugar

½ cup dry red wine

½ teaspoon cayenne pepper

4 sweet Italian sausages, cooked and sliced

1 ½ pounds rigatoni cooked al dente

1 cup fontina cheese, shredded

1 cup Parmesan cheese, shredded

In large deep skillet, put in olive oil, garlic, onion, and herbs and cook on med high heat for about 3 min.

Then put in all the cans of tomatoes and water, mix well with whisk.

Add salt, pepper, sugar, wine, and cayenne pepper.

Boil, then quickly turn heat to simmer and cover for 1 hour, mixing once or twice. Add the italian sausage.

Turn oven on to 350 and place the cooked rigatoni in a deep baking dish. Pour the sauce on top. Mix so all is covered. Sprinkle on cheeses.

Bake until the cheese melts.

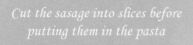

Cut the sasage into slices before putting them in the pasta

Barlo

Serve Mangiare

Great Family Pasta – Frittata Style

1 lb. of pasta, elbow macaroni, cooked al dente

1 large onion, chopped

4 teaspoons of olive oil

4 tablespoons of butter

12 large eggs

6 tomatoes, chopped

4 tablespoons of heavy cream

Salt and pepper

2 cups Gruyere cheese, grated

Heat oven to 400.

In oven-proof frying pan, place in ½ the butter and olive oil on med high on stove.

Sauté onions until golden.

In bowl, stir together eggs, tomatoes, cream, salt, and pepper.

Stir in the pasta and add the remaining butter and pour the egg mixture in.

Cook for about a minute until it bubbles then take off heat and put into the oven for 40 min.

Then take out of oven and loosen the edges by shaking the pan.

Place the Gruyere cheese on and place under the boiler for no more than a minute.

Take out of oven, let set for 15 minutes, and then cut and serve. Great with a loaf of Italian bread.

Serve
Mangiare

ROSALIE SCHWAMB

Easy Lasagna Roll Ups

1 box of lasagna pasta

1 large jar of sauce, either Alfredo sauce or Tomato sauce, or use one of my recipes

2 lbs of ground beef

2 cloves of garlic

1 large onion, chopped

2 tablespoons of Italian herbs

2 eggs

1 carton of ricotta cheese

½ cup of chopped parsley

1 cup parmesan cheese

2 cups of mozzarella cheese (but wait to use until lasagna has been cooking for 25 minutes)

In sauté pan, brown the beef and then drain.

Saute the garlic, onions and Italian herbs in 2 tablespoons of butter.

When lightly brown, take off the heat and mix in the drained beef.

In mixing bowl, stir in the 2 eggs, ricotta cheese, parsley, and parmesan cheese.

Mix together the beef mixture and the cheese mixture.

Place 2 tablespoons on a lasagna noodle. Spread down and then rollup.

Do that until all rolled. Place in 13x9 inch baking dish, seam side down.

Pour the sauce over the noodles and bake at 350 for 25 minutes then add the mozzarella and cook for another 15 to 20 minutes.

Serve with Italian bread and salad.

Mama Schwamb's recipes

Family favorite, my Godson Jack loves this dish

Serve Mangiare

Rosemary Schwamb, she is my Auntie Rosie. She can cook anything and make it taste wonderful. She is a recording artist, a singer by heart.

She has a great family, and her husband My uncle Bud was the best! Here is auntie Rosie on a trip we went on together posing like a star.

S paghetti Gumach

1 ½ pounds ground beef

1 large onions, chopped

1 tablespoon parsley, minced

4 stalks celery, chopped

A dash paprika

1 tablespoon dry onion soup

A dash of pepper

A dash of cayenne pepper

1 28-ounce can whole tomatoes, crushed

1 8-ounce can tomato sauce

2 dashes sugar

1 pound spaghetti, cooked al dente

Saute and drain the beef.

In the same pan, cook onions and celery until tender. Add the paprika, onion soup, pepper, cayenne, crushed tomatoes, tomato sauce and 2 dashes of sugar.

Let simmer for 30 min.

Cook the pasta and drain.

Place pasta in serving bowl and pour meat mixture over the pasta.

Auntie Rosie's recipe

Barolo

Serve Mangiare

*I*talian Mac & Cheese

1 pound pasta any kind

Salt and pepper

4 ounces creamy havarti cheese or any kind you have on hand

6 ounces valvetta cheese

½ cup milk

¼ cup dry Italian bread crumbs

3 tablespoons butter

Cook pasta until al dente.

In sauce pan, put in the cheeses, milk, and 2 tbs butter. Cook until melted, stirring constantly.

Mix into pasta.

In small bowl, melt 1 tbs butter and then add the bread crumbs. Mix and spread all over pasta mixture.

Bake at 350 for 20 min.

This is a staple in all homes & so easy to make.

You can also add vegetables and meat to this dish, its a meal.

Serve Mangiare

ROSALIE SCHWAMB

Pasta Rosemary Fagioli

1 tablespoon fresh rosemary, chopped

¼ teaspoon red pepper flakes or cayenne pepper

1 onion, chopped

5 cloves garlic, minced

2 strips bacon, chopped

⅛ cup olive oil

3 25-ounce cans chunk tomatoes

2 15-ounce cans northern beans

2 15-ounce cans red kidney beans

2 bay leaves

½ cup Parmesan cheese

12 ounces pasta shells

¼ cup fresh parsley, chopped

Salt and pepper

Put olive oil in large pot over med heat. Add the bacon and let it brown then add the rosemary, pepper flakes, onion, and garlic.

Cook for about 4 minutes. Add the tomatoes. Cook for 4 minutes, then add the beans, 6 cups of water, the bay leaves, and parmesan cheese.

Cover and bring to a boil then reduce heat and let simmer for 30 minutes.

Then bring it back up to a boil and add the pasta. Cook until al dente or about 8-10 minutes.

Remove the bay leaves and add the parsley, salt, and pepper to taste and more Parmesan cheese if desired.

Warm, hearty dish

Serve Mangiare

Pasta and Peas

1 lb bow tie pasta cooked until al dente

1 bag frozen peas

½ bag frozen carrots

4 ounces cream cheese

4 ounces mascarpone cheese

Salt and pepper

Cook pasta and drain. In same pot, place the thawed peas and carrots.

Add the softened cream cheese, mascarpone cheese, salt, and pepper.

To your liking, add cherry tomatoes, shrimp or crab

Serve Mangiare

Rosalie Schwamb

*I*talian Sausage with Tortellini

1 tbsp olive oil
1 tbs butter
4 Italian sausages
2 cloves garlic, minced
cup onion, chopped
28 oz can of cubed tomatoes
¼ cup tomato paste

¼ cup red wine
2 tbsp chopped basil
1 tsp dried Italian herbs
¼ tsp red pepper flakes
1 green pepper, cut into chucks
1 lb of any store
bought tortellini

Cook the Italian sausages either in a pan or oven, pan is quicker.

Put sausages in pan with a cup of water. Bring to boil, reduce, and drain water. Cook for another 3-4 minutes, turning. Then remove from pan.

Let sit for 5 minutes then cut into slices.

In the same pan, put in the oil and butter and sauté the garlic and onions.

Cook until tender, not browned, about 3-4 minutes, then stir in the tomatoes paste.

Add the wine, basil, herbs and pepper flakes. Then add the sausage and green peppers. Bring to a boil, reduce the heat, cover, and let simmer for about 20 minutes.

While that is simmering, make the pasta.

Drain and pour into serving platter.

Place the sausage sauce on top and garnish with more fresh basil and parmesan cheese.

Serve Mangiare

M anicotti

Filling:

2 cups ricotta cheese

½ cup Parmesan cheese

2 tablespoons parsley

1 ¾ cups mozzarella cheese

1 pound cooked meat (beef, sausage, pork, turkey or chicken)

Batter:

1 cup water

A pinch of salt

1 cup flour

4 eggs

Mix together the filling mixture except for 1 cup of the mozzarella. Set aside.

Mix together, with a wire wisk, all batter ingredients. In a non-stick skillet, wipe the inside with a paper towel and some oil. Spoon batter until thin, cook until top is shinny, flip and ready to stuff and bake.

Stuff the manicotti one by one place in baking dish. Place sauce on top of manicotti and the remainder of mozzarella. Bake at 350 for 30 min covered with foil.

*Serve
Mangiare*

Pesto Sauce

2 cloves garlic, chopped

1 cup basil

¼ cup parsley

3 tablespoons pine nuts

4 tablespoons Parmesan cheese

¼ cup olive oil

Place garlic, basil, parsley, nuts and parmesan cheese
in food processor. Pulse slowly.
Add olive oil and salt to taste.

Savignion Blanc

*Serve
Mangiare*

Mediterranean Sauce

1 tbsp Olive oil

⅓ cup onion chopped

2 cloves Garlic minced

28 oz can Italian tomatoes

14 oz can tomato sauce

14 oz can tomato paste

2 tbsp sugar

3 tbsp Italian seasoning

¼ tsp cayenne pepper

¼ cup red wine

1 lb Pasta any kind

Heat the oil in large sauce pan over medium heat.

Add the onions and garlic and cook until tender, but not brown, about 3 minutes.

Add the unstrained tomatoes, tomato sauce and the tomato paste.

Add 1 cup of water and whisk. Then add the sugar, seasoning, cayenne pepper and wine.

Bring to a boil and then let simmer for about 40 minutes.

Great served with olives over the pasta.

Serve
Mangiare

ROSALIE SCHWAMB

*S*tuffed Italian Sausage Shells

8 ounces italian sauage, cooked

1 large green bell peppers, chopped

1 large onions, chopped

2 carrots, chopped

2 stalks celery, chopped

24 ounces marinara sauce

1 15-ounce container ricotta cheese

8 ounces mozzarella cheese

½ cup Parmesan cheese

1 package pasta shells, jumbo cooked al dente

Preheat oven to 350. Coat 3 quart baking pan with cooking spray.

In skillet, put in the onions, carrots, peppers, and celery. Cook on medium heat until lightly golden.

In a bowl, combine the sausage, the ricotta cheese, and onion mixture. Mix in the parmesan cheese.

Stuff each shell. After all stuffed, pour over the marinara sauce .

Place in oven for 25 minutes covered with foil. Take off the cover, put on the mozzarella, and bake for 10-15 more minutes.

Barolo

Serve Mangiare

Pizza Sauce

1 14.5-oz can tomato paste

2 ½ cups water

⅓ cup olive oil

4 cloves garlic, minced

Salt and pepper

4 tablespoons pizza herbs (or you can make your own)

1 tbsp oregano

1 tbsp basil

1 tbsp rosemary

1 tbsp red pepper flakes

Mix all and put into fridge. Best to leave overnight.

Good to cover 2 pizzas

ROSALIE SCHWAMB

S paghetti Sauce

2 tablespoons olive oil

5 cloves garlic, minced

1 small onions, chopped

1 tablespoon itialian seasoning dry herbs
 (your favorite blend)

1 12-ounce can tomato paste

1 14.5 ounce can diced tomatoes

1 29-ounce can tomato sauce

1 cup water

Salt and pepper

⅛ cup sugar

½ teaspoon cayenne pepper

In large pot on med heat, put in olive oil, garlic, onion, and herbs for about 3 min.

Put in all the cans of tomatoes and water, mix well with whisk.

Add salt and pepper, then the sugar, wine and cayenne pepper.

Boil then quickly turn heat to simmer and let it simmer for an hour.

Watch the onions and garlic carefully, so they dont burn

Serve Mangiare

Marinara Sauce

2 28-oz cans of crushed tomatoes, seasoned preferred

2 tablespoons olive oil

1 med onions, chopped

2 cloves garlic, chopped

1 teaspoon italian herbs

⅓ cup dry red wine

Salt and pepper

1 teaspoon sugar

3 tablespoons sweet basil, fresh, chopped

Heat oil in skillet over medium heat. Add onions and cook until soft and golden.

Add garlic and herbs and cook for 1 more minute.

Add the 2 cans of tomatoes, cook for 10 minutes.

Add in wine, salt, pepper, and sugar. Cook for 5 minutes.

Turn to simmer for 10 minutes.

Serve over pasta or any kind of meat. Sprinkle with the cut basil.

Barolo

Serve Mangiare

ROSALIE SCHWAMB

Uncooked Tomato Sauce

2 cloves garlic, minced

8 basil leaves, chopped

¼ cup parsley leaves, chopped

½ tsp sea salt

4 large tomatoes, peeled, deseeded, and diced

½ cup olive oil

Mix all together and serve over a pound of any type of pasta, hot or cold.

Makes 2 cups of sauce.

In place of the regular tomatoes, use cherry tomatoes cut in half Oh la la!

Serve Mangiare

Dolcetto

*E*asy Fettuccine Alfredo Sauce

1 lb Fettuccine

1 cup of half-and-half or heavy whipping cream

¼ cup butter

1 cup Parmesan cheese

¾ teas salt

2 cloves garlic, minced

3 tablespoon fresh basil, chopped

½ teaspoon pepper

In large sauce pan, boil water for the pasta.

Reduce the heat slightly, boil until al dente. Cook according to package directions, drain, and return the pasta back to the pot.

Add the half-and-half, butter, cheese, salt and garlic.

Toss gently until coated. Put on a big platter and sprinkle with pepper and basil.

I love to use this sauce as lasagna sauce instead of red sauce.

Serve Mangiare

ROSALIE SCHWAMB

Potatoes

Potato Benilli

2 lbs potatoes, any kind, cooked and mashed

½ cup onions, any kind, chopped

1 cup Parmesan cheese, grated

1 cup bread crumbs

2 tablespoons fresh basil and oregano

½ tablespoon nutmeg, grated

2 tablespoons olive oil

1 tablespoon butter

Mix all and place in med high skillet with the olive oil and butter.

Brown on both sides, 2 min each side.

Serve.

Recipe is the family staple passed down from both sides of my grandparents families. They all came from Sicily, Palermo, grandfather and Santalia grandmother.

Serve Mangiare

ROSALIE SCHWAMB

My Auntie Sara, the most wonderful lady in the world.
She never had a bad word to say about anyone.

*I*talian Omelette (Frittata or Frochia)

2 potatoes cleaned and thinly sliced

½ onion chopped

½ cup of drained spinach (this is optional)

6 eggs

2 tablespoon oil

1 tablespoon of butter

Pinch of sugar and cinnamon

Salt and pepper to taste

In sauté pan on medium heat, put in the oil and butter, and sauté the potatoes when lightly browned.

Add the onions and spinach, sauté for about 4 minutes. You may need to add a little more oil, not too much, then add the eggs with a tablespoon of water, add the sugar, cinnamon, salt and pepper.

Cook till bubbles and place a large dish to flip, then place back into sauté pan for about 1 to 2 minutes and place dish again over pan and there you go.

Cut into pie slices and serve with a great loaf of Italian bread.

This recipe is from my Auntie Sarah, she would come over to my Nanu's house and they would go back and forth on who was going to flip the Frochia.

Uncle Joe, Uncle John, Auntie Beauty, Auntie Sarah, Auntie Lucy. They are kindest and most loving.

Serve Mangiare

ROSALIE SCHWAMB

Scalloped Potatoes and Prosciutto

2 tablespoons butter
2 tablespoons flour
1 cup heavy cream
½ cup milk
Salt and pepper

1 tablespoon butter
2 onions thinly sliced
4 potatoes sliced
1 ½ cups ham and/or
6 slices prosciutto chopped

Preheat oven to 350. Butter a baking dish.

In a saucepan, melt 2 tablespoons of butter over medium high heat.

Stir in flour and cook for 1 minute.

Remove saucepan from heat and whisk in milk and heavy cream. Return pan to heat and bring to a simmer while stirring.

When sauce has thickened, remove from heat, season with salt and pepper and set aside. In a skillet, cook onions in melted butter until golden brown.

Season with salt and pepper. In bottom of baking dish, spread some sauce and top with half of the potatoes, half of the onions, ham and or prosciutto, cheese and half of the sauce, salt and pepper.

Continue layering potatoes, onions, ham and or prosciutto, half of the sauce, salt and pepper ending with the remaining cheese on top.

Bake for 45 minutes or until golden and bubbly.

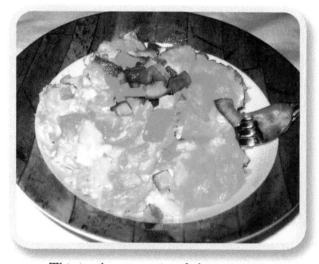

This is a heat warming dish to serve just alone with bread and wine.

Serve
Mangiare

Potato Wedges

3 pounds potatoes, leave skins on and slice

4 tablespoons olive oil

Salt and pepper

1 tablespoon paprika

1 package onion soup mix, grounded up more

In bowl, place onion soup mix and potatoes. Turn until all coated.

Place potatoes on cookie sheet sprayed in olive oil.

Sprinkle paprika, salt, and pepper on top of potatoes.

Bake at 425 for 30 to 45 min until tender and brown.

To make Italian style in place of onion mix 2 tablespoons of my Italian herbs.

The potatoes can be placed on top of mashed potatoes to serve.

Serve Mangiare

Rosalie Schwamb

Patate (Potatoes with Cream)

3 gloves garlic, minced

2 tablespoons butter

3 pounds potatoes any kind, sliced

3 cups heavy cream

½ cup cream creme fraiche or sour cream

2 tablespoons flour

2 teaspoons thyme, fresh, finely chopped

2 teaspoons basil, fresh, finely chopped

1 cup onions, any kind

Salt and pepper

Preheat oven to 350.

In 3 quart baking dish, rub 1 clove of garlic and 1 tbsp butter all over. Take sliced potatoes and put into the dish.

In sauce pan, combine the rest of the garlic and butter, the heavy cream, the creme fraiche or sour cream, and the flour, herbs salt, and pepper.

Bring to boil. Stir constantly until the mixture thickens.

Pour over the potatoes and bake uncovered for 1 hour.

This is Sarah Fina's favorite dish.

Serve Mangiare

Desserts

Chocolate Chip Chewys

1 ¼ cups granulated sugar

1 ¼ cups packed brown sugar

1 ½ cups butter or margarine, softened

2 teaspoons vanilla

3 eggs

4 ¼ ups all-purpose flour

2 teaspoons baking soda

½ teaspoon salt

1 to 2 bags (12 oz each)
semisweet chocolate chips (2 to 4 cups)

Heat oven to 375°F. In large bowl with electric mixer, beat granulated sugar, brown sugar and butter until light and fluffy. Beat in vanilla and eggs until well blended. Beat in flour, baking soda and salt. Stir in chocolate chips.

On ungreased cookie sheets, drop dough by rounded tablespoonfuls, 2 inches apart.

Bake 8 to 10 minutes or until light golden brown. Cool 1 minute; remove from cookie sheets to cooling racks.

Serve
Mangiare

$\mathcal{F}$ocaccia Blueberry Style

½ cup sugar

1 tablespoon lemon zest

3 cups flour

1 package yeast rapid rise

¾ tablespoon salt

1 ¼ cups milk

1 large eggs eighty beaten

½ stick butter

2 cups blueberries

Place sugar and lemon zest in food prossessor until finely ground, making lemon sugar. In large bowl, whisk ⅓ cup of lemon sugar, 3 cups of flour, yeast, and salt until blended.

Heat milk in microwave on high for 1 minute. Add flour mixture with egg and butter. Mix until it becomes soft and sticky. Put down on floured surface and knead for 2 mintues. Put back in mixing bowl, let rest for 10 minutes.

Line a large baking sheet with parchment paper, divide dough in half. Roll one piece of dough out into a rectangle and scatter half the blueberry mixture and half of the lemon sugar mixture on to the dough. Roll the other piece of dough out into a triangle, smaller than the first one. Put it on top of the first one and press the edges together and tuck under, like a loaf. Cover with a sheet of greased plastic wrap. Place in warm area for 1 hour. Let rise.

Heat oven to 350 degrees. Poke into the top surface of loaf and scatter the remaining blueberries and lemon sugar. Bake 25-30 minutes until golden brown. Cool on wire rack. Serve warm.

Apples can be used in place of blueberries, then you wan to put the cinnamon in place if the lemon.

Serve Mangiare

Rosalie Schwamb

*L*emon Mascarpone Cupcakes

¼ cup of mascarpone

2 teaspoons of lemon extract

½ cup butter soft

2 eggs

½ buttermilk

¼ cup milk

1 teaspoon vanilla

2 cups flour

1 tablespoon baking powder

1 teaspoon salt

½ teaspoon of mascarpone cheese mixture

In small bowl mix together mascarpone and lemon extract put in fridge for later use.

Beat together butter, eggs, buttermilk, milk, and vanilla.

Mix in slowly: flour, baking powder, and saldt.

Line cupcake pan.

Place batter ¾ full.

Place in mascarpone cheese mixture in each cupcake.

Bake at 350 till spings back about 12-15 minutes
.

To drizzle with lemon frosting:

1 cup powdered sugar 1 tablespoon milk and

1 teaspoon lemon extract add more powdered

sugar if you want it less smooth

Serve
Mangiare

*S*trawberry Pie with Marscarponi Cheese & Cream

2 sheets refrigerated pie crust

1 egg white to brush on pie

1 tablespoon sugar to sprinkle on crust

6 cups strawberries hulled and sliced only in half

½ cup sugar

3 tablespoons cornstarch

Pinch salt

1 cup whipped cream

½ cup mascarpone cheese, soften

Preheat the oven to 400.

Roll out 1 sheet of the pie crust and put in a 9-inch pie plate. Set aside.

In a medium bowl, mix together all of the filling ingredients: strawberries, sugar, cornstarch and salt. Pour into the crust.

Put the other sheet of pie crust over the the filled pie and crimp down edging. Brush top with egg whites and sprinkle with sugar.

Bake the pie for 25 minutes at 400 then reduce the temperature to 350 and bake until the top is golden brown, about 30 more minutes.

Let cool before serving with Strawberry Whipped Cream mixed with mascarpone cheese.

This is Sarah Fina's favorite dish.

Serve Mangiare

ROSALIE SCHWAMB

Papa Schwamb's Banana Cake

1 package yellow cake mix

3 eggs

4 bananas, mashed

1 cup sour cream

¼ cup applesauce

1 8-ounce package cream cheese, softened

1 stick butter, softened

1 16-ounce box powdered sugar

1 cup walnuts or any kind you like, finely chopped

Heat oven to 350

Beat cake mix, eggs, bananas, sour cream, and apple sauce on low until moistened then on medium until well blended. Pour into greased and floured 13 x 9 inch pan.

Bake 35 minutes or until toothpick comes out clean. Cool completely.

Beat cream cheese and butter until well blended gradually adding the powdered sugar.

Frost cooled cake. Sprinkle nuts if you desire.

You may also take cooled cake, cut it in half, and frost middle, tops, and sides and put on the nuts as desired. Serve.

This is my daughter Rosalia's favorite. I make it for her birthday every year.

Can use 2 8-inch rounds, and decorate with nuts.

Serve Mangiare

My Apple Pie

½ cup sugar

¼ cup flour

1 teaspoon cinnamon

⅛ teaspoon allspice

6 cups peeled and sliced apples, any kind

Pastry for pie

In mixing bowl, combine sugar, flour, cinnamon, and allspice.

Add apples and put into pie crust. Put 2 pieces of butter on apples.

Put other pie crust on top. Cut slits into pie and brush with egg and sprinkle cinnamon sugar on top.

Bake at 375 for 25-35 minutes or until knife slides with ease.

I go the the apple orchard and get a big bushel of apples, and my daughter Rosalie comes over and we make tons of pies that afternoon.

Serve Mangiare

Dream Sickle Cheese Cake

2 8-oz box of cream cheese softened

1 8-oz tub of whipped cream

⅓ cup sugar

1 tablespoon orange liqueur

1 orange, just the juice

1 lemon peel, fine

1 orange peel, fine

1 graham cracker pie crust

Mix cream cheese, whipped cream, sugar, the juice from the orange, the orange liqueur and the lemon and orange peels.

Spread on the graham cracker pie crust.

Can garnish with some mint and some orange swirl.

This tastes like summer

Serve Mangiare

Quick Cobbler

½ cup butter soft

2 eggs

½ buttermilk

¼ cup milk

1 teaspoon vanilla

2 cups flour

1 tablespoon baking powder

1 teaspoon salt

2 cans of pie filling any kind

Beat together butter, eggs, buttermilk, milk, and vanilla.

Mix in slowly: flour, baking powder, and salt.

Place pie filling on bottom of 9x13 pan.

Then place the cake mixture down and bake at 350 till knife comes out clean.

To make drizzeld icing: 1 cup powdered sugar and 2 tablespoon of milk at a time for your liking.

*Serve
Mangiare*

ROSALIE SCHWAMB

Cheese Cake

2 8-oz box of cream cheese, softened

1 8-oz tub of whipped cream

⅓ cup sugar

1 teaspoon rum

1 graham cracker pie crust

Mix together cream cheese, whipped cream, sugar, and rum.

Spread into prepared graham cracker pie crust.

Can be served or topped with any berries.

Berries everywhere

Serve Mangiare

Banana Split Pie

1 pie shell baked and cooled (can use graham cracker crust)

6 ounces caramel topping

2 to 3 bananas, sliced

2 cups of vanilla ice cream

1 cup whipped cream

¼ cup powdered sugar

1 cup semisweet chocolate chips

1 teaspoon oils

Spoon caramel into center of cooled crust; gently spread to edge. Thinly slice bananas; arrange ice cream over the carmel.

In medium bowl, beat whipping cream and powdered sugar with electric mixer on high speed until stiff peaks form. Spread over ice cream.

In small resealable freezer plastic bag, place chocolate chips and oil; seal bag. Microwave on high for 30 seconds; knead bag to mix melted chips and unmelted chips. Microwave 15 to 30 seconds longer or until all chips are melted and smooth.

Snip off tiny corner of bag. Pipe melted chocolate mixture over whipped cream. Store pie in refrigerator.

Graham pie mixture: 1 ¼ cups graham crackers, 3 tablespoons sugar, ⅓ cup melted butter can bake for 10 minutes at 325 if you want the crust to be firmer.

Serve Mangiare

ROSALIE SCHWAMB

This is my Great Nana Rosa, who is the head of the famliy, with her Children, Jerome, Frank, Marie, Sara. We are a close family with losts of love.

Cassata alla Siciliana

Filling:
2 cups of mascarpone cheese
¼ cup ricotta cheese
¼ cup sugar
2/3 cup of pistachios
2/3 cup chocolate chips

Cake:
6 eggs, separated

1 ⅓ cup of sugar
Half of 1 lemon juice
1 tablespoon of almond extract
Pinch of salt
1 ¼ cups of flour
Frosting
2 cups of heavy cream
¼ cup sugar
1 tablespoon of lemon peel

Start with the filling: mix all together, cover, and place in fridge.

Preheat oven to 350.

Beat the egg yolks, gradually adding the ½ cup of sugar. Add the lemon juice and the almond extract. Continue beating until mixture is frothy and almost lemon colored.

Set aside and in another bowl mix the egg whites until foamy, gradually add the other ½ cup of sugar. Beat until stiff. Fold in the egg yolk mixture a little at a time alternating with the flour and salt until all folded together.

Pour batter into butter and floured pans, square or round. Bake for 25-30 minutes or until toothpick comes out clean.

When cooled, take out filling. Place one cake on plate, fill the layer, and place the other one on top.

Frosting: Mix the cream, sugar, and peel then frost the cake. You can use cake frosting for this cake also and put food coloring in the frosting.

My mama, Josephine Taglialavora's recipe

In place of the frosting, you can use cake frosting and put in food colors, in this instance I also placed cannoli around the cake.

Serve Mangiare

ROSALIE SCHWAMB

My Nana Rosalie with my mothers Cassata cake
at Christmas time.

My passion for cooking began when I was a little girl. I was born in Milwaukee, Wisconsin and grew up living next door to my Grandparents. My grandma (Nana) had a large fresh herb garden in her yard along with a huge vegetable garden. I would spend many afternoons with her picking bundles of herbs that she would use to make dinners. My grandmother would pick the herbs, pass them to me and ask me what I thought they smelled like before telling me what the names of the herbs were. This was one of my favorite pastimes as a little girl. After we gathered the herbs we would go into the house and cook with them. My grandmother would teach me how to flavor the meals using the herbs we just picked. She and my grandfather's family came from Sicily and spoke mostly Italian in their home in the early years. My grandmother would talk to me in Italian as she taught me how to cook. I learned so much from my grandparents and the values and traditions that I learned is something I pass to my children every day. My family moved to Greenfield, a suburb of Milwaukee. I met my soul mate Mark Schwamb while attending high school and married him right after graduation. Soon we had our first child, Mark II and three years later we had our second child Rosalia. I have always been very passionate about cooking and six years ago my mother and I set out on this journey to write a cook book. I was so excited about the idea of passing down my family's traditions and secrets that were taught to me as a young girl. My mother Josephine and I had a very similar style when it came to cooking. Of course we wanted our food to be delicious, but we also wanted our food to be inventive. We used creative ways of using herbs and fresh ingredients to make beautiful food, hence the name of our book, "Bella Mangiare" Unfortunately, five years ago my mothers dream was cut short when she passed away from cancer. Honoring her memory has given me the strength to finish this dream we both started. I am delighted to share with you my family's traditions and our passion for cooking with this book of fresh and creative recipes to warm your heart.

ROSALIE SCHWAMB

Printed in the USA
CPSIA information can be obtained
at www.ICGtesting.com
LVHW061106151123
763879LV00015BA/116